The SCIENCE & ART of TENNIS

by

JULIO YACUB

DRAWINGS BY HENCHE SILBERSTEIN

HATS
OFF™

THE ULTIMATE PICTORIAL MANUAL FOR SINGLES

Published by Hats Off Books™
610 East Delano Street, Suite 104
Tucson, Arizona 85705

ISBN: 1-58736-212-0
LCCN: 2003093526

FOREWORD

I've known Julio for many years and feel you would be hard pressed to find someone so committed to the game. He understands the skills and strategy of the game and has poured his heart and soul into this book. You'll find the reading to be informative and the unique artwork enjoyable to study.

He shares my intense passion for teaching students of all ages and I believe that comes through to the reader. As an author myself, I can appreciate the effort he has put forth to compile all this information and I commend him on his end product.

Nick Bollettieri
President and Founder
Bollettieri Tennis Academy

TABLE OF CONTENTS

PREFACE

As a self-taught tennis player, I always looked for books that could help me improve my game. Most of the books that I read were long, wordy, and complicated. In college, I had the same problem: books, books, books, but none to my taste, simple but in-depth. I always needed to make outlines to focus on the specific things I wanted to work on. It is true that a good way of learning is to make your own outline, but sometimes we need them ready in order to concentrate on the goals without getting lost in words. This book is written in outline form, and it is simple to follow. You can even take it down to the court and concentrate on any stroke simply by taking a glimpse at that specific page.

The Science & Art of Tennis is designed for visual learners and students of the game who look for simplicity without cutting corners, but it is not picture-perfect. In this ever-changing game, where there are many stances, several ways to take the racquet back, hit the ball, and follow through, it would be impossible for me to include everything. That's why I laid out this book as a guide, so you can understand how biomechanics work in tennis, and, with the help of your local pro, I hope you can improve your tennis game dramatically.

Even though the drawings and diagrams are shown from a right-handed player's perspective, any left-handed player can interpret them by using a mirror image view. I included side and front views for most of the strokes so the conversion would be easier. Also, to better understand the court diagrams, place yourself in it or imagine that you are on the court playing that particular pattern (instead of just thinking player A and player B). Finally, when using the terms "he" and "his," I imply, by all means, "she" and "hers."

Julio Yacub

ACKNOWLEDGMENT

I must mention that without the help of many people I would not be the person and player that I am today. I would like to thank my mentors, Nick Bollettieri, Vic Braden, and Dennis Van Der Meer, for their continuous contributions to the game and my tennis life.

A special thanks to Jack Groppel and Jim Loehr, who enlightened me to the realms of sport psychology and biomechanics (when they talk...I listen!). I would also like to extend my warmest gratitude to my first coach Ron Steele, former head coach of the Israeli Davis Cup team, for taking me under his wing when I was nothing. Thanks to the USTA High Performance Coaching Program team, especially to Nick Saviano and Paul Lubbers, for raising the stakes in American coaching. Sincere appreciation to my friends John Lapham and Claudio Yamus...and to all my students for sticking with me all these years...you have been the source of my inspiration.

Finally, and most importantly, I would like to thank my family, especially my wife Maura and my mother Henche Silberstein, without whose contributions and support this book would be just a fantasy.

LEGEND

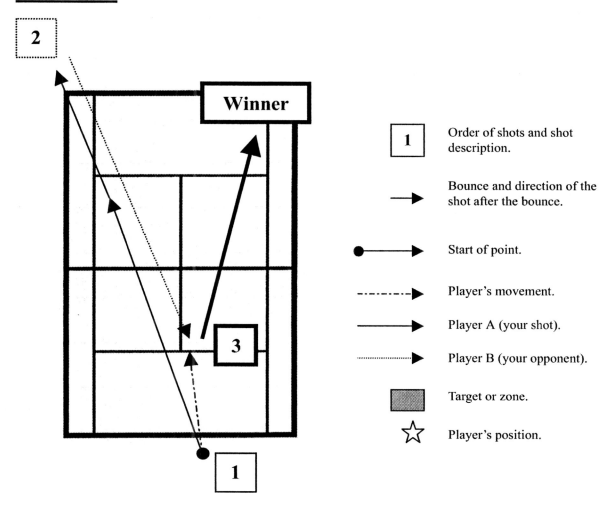

1	Order of shots and shot description.
→	Bounce and direction of the shot after the bounce.
•——→	Start of point.
·—·—·—►	Player's movement.
———►	Player A (your shot).
········►	Player B (your opponent).
▨	Target or zone.
☆	Player's position.

NOTE:

- All diagrams are shown from a right-handed player's perspective, and, unless mentioned, all patterns are identical from the ad or deuce courts, consequently, easily convertible for left-handed players as well as for planning a strategy from both courts. (Patterns are based on geometry of the court and percentage, not player's strength or weakness).
- All "order of shots and shot description" boxes are border coded with the respective shot (line) for easy recognition.

CHAPTER 1

<u>INTRO TO THE GAME</u>

STANCES

<u>STANCES</u>
Forehand and Backhand

All stances derive from an athletic, ready position. From this neutral position, not only will you be ready to move in any direction with quickness and effectiveness (balanced start), but most importantly, the "kinetic body chain" will be maximized (rhythm and power production as well as control enhancement and injury prevention).

While most professional players choose the open stance (mostly for forehands) because of its quick preparation and recovery, you should balance the specs of each stance, experiment with them, and choose your own. Keep in mind that a good player is flexible enough to adapt to any tactical situation, and, therefore, proficiency in all stances is a good asset.

The Kinetic Body Chain

All Strokes

The kinetic body chain refers to the segments of the body that act as a chain (body links) in order to produce energy. Starting with the knee extension, ground forces are generated ("for every action there is an equal and opposite reaction") and successfully transferred from link to link until they reach the ball.

The body link system consists of (in order of execution):
1. Knee extension
2. Hip rotation
3. Trunk rotation
4. Shoulder and arm rotation
5. Elbow extension (internal rotation)
6. Wrist flexion

In order to generate with efficiency (avoiding injury) the maximum amount of power and control, the body links must be in coordination (timing), meaning that the body link system should be kept in sequence for all strokes starting from the ground up (knees to wrist), without omitting any segment, and without the use of extra body parts (unnecessary elbow motion or too much wrist).

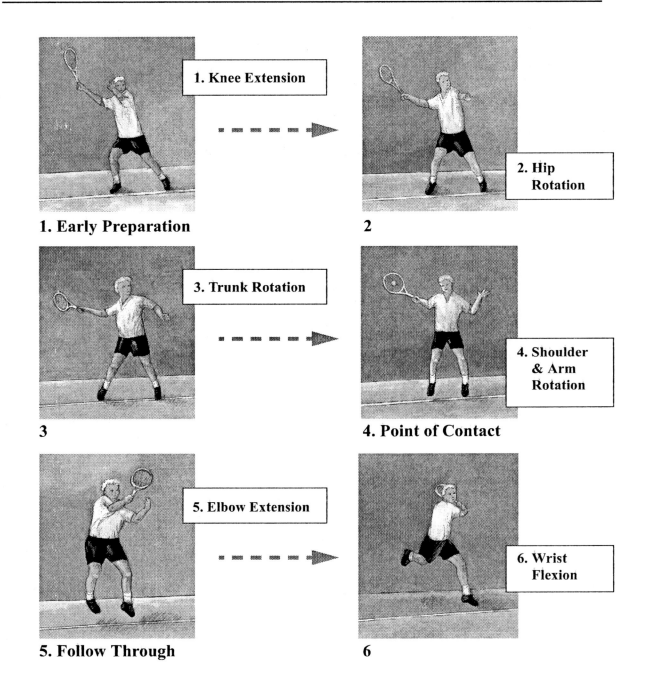

1. Early Preparation

2

3

4. Point of Contact

5. Follow Through

6

1. Knee Extension

2. Hip Rotation

3. Trunk Rotation

4. Shoulder & Arm Rotation

5. Elbow Extension

6. Wrist Flexion

READY POSITION (NEUTRAL)

- Feet shoulder-width apart.
- Knees bent about 30 degrees. Lowering your body (center of gravity) will prepare your leg muscles to react quicker as well as set you up into a balanced position.
- Head up and body weight slightly forward (on the balls of your feet).
- Racquet is held at the center of your body, out in front, high but below eye level.
- Free hand holds the racquet at its throat.
- Be relaxed but alert and aware of opponent's next shot.

OPEN STANCE

Advantages:

- Quicker preparation (for groundstrokes, and especially needed for quick return of serves).
- Quicker recovery (back foot is ready to push to the "Recovery Site").[1]
- Better court coverage.
- Excellent deception of shot aiming (keeps opponent guessing).
- Ease on crosscourt shots.
- Enables you to keep the front side of the body clear throughout the shot (no restrictions in rotating the shoulders and hips).
- Easy to slide and reach on clay courts, especially on stretch shots.
- Excellent racquet head acceleration.

Disadvantages:

- Requires upper body flexibility to rotate the shoulders while keeping the hips open (especially for backhands).
- Requires powerful leg action due to the reduced weight transfer (no step into the ball like the square stance).
- Requires quicker footwork to get closer to the ball. A two-handed open stance shot requires you to get closer to the ball to make contact, compared to a square or closed stance. This makes a big difference on running wide shots.
- Difficult to hit down-the-line shots.
- Requires a strong arm and wrist for a good swing and snap.
- Lower percentage shot because of the extra use of arm and wrist.

SQUARE STANCE

Advantages:

- Excellent weight transfer due to the forward step.
- Good power production (use of kinetic body chain).
- Better aiming by ease to follow through forward to the target.
- Easy to set up the backhand (especially the one-handed).
- Overall comfortable feel.
- Ease of down-the-line shots.

Disadvantages:

- One extra step needed for recovery.
- Harder to keep good balance.

CLOSED STANCE

Advantages:

- Easy to hit running wide shots and passing shots.
- Ease of defensive slice.

Disadvantages:

- Inefficient weight transfer.
- Loss of energy (power) due to sideways-locked hips (no hip rotation).
- Harder to maintain balance due to the weak foundation (foot position).
- Diminished racquet head acceleration.
- Slower to recover.
- Difficult to hit crosscourt shots.

[1] See *Recovering* in Chapter 1, **"Anticipation and Footwork"**

BACKSWING STYLES

BACKSWING STYLES
Flat or Topspin

Forehand and Backhand

Backswing should be considered a style of play, and each player should develop his own as it is practiced. All backswing styles, however, have the same basic and simple foundation: from the ready position[1] / split step / react, turn your shoulders (unit turn), and the racquet automatically goes back. The difference lies in the size of the backswing loop, or whether there is a loop at all.

1. Split Step   **2. Shoulder Turn**   **3. Backswing Style**

1. Split Step   **2. Shoulder Turn**   **3. Backswing Style**

The most common backswings are:

STRAIGHT-BACK

- Easy and quick backswing, but not much spin production. Racquet head acceleration is generated mostly from the forward arm swing. Therefore, a strong arm is needed. Used mostly for quick return of serves and shots hit on the run, like passing shots.

1   *Side View*   **2**

DOWNWARD BACKSWING

- Just like the straight-back backswing, this one is quick and fairly easy. Good topspin production, but if hit late it could become a scoop (racquet hits under the ball, leaving with an upward trajectory and no spin). Make sure, if you use this kind of backswing, not to continue further back than necessary (tip of the racquet should point back), otherwise, the racquet will come up behind you, and a slice (underspin) shot will be produced.

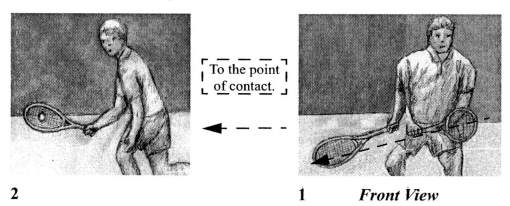

2   **1**   *Front View*

LOOP BACKSWING

- Choice of most of the pros. Excellent rhythm, acceleration, and topspin production. Racquet is taken back with a high loop. As you are getting ready for the forward swing, the racquet drops down easily, thanks to gravity (racquet weight), and accelerates to the point of contact.

- **Compact "C" Loop (On the backhand, looks like an inverted "C")**

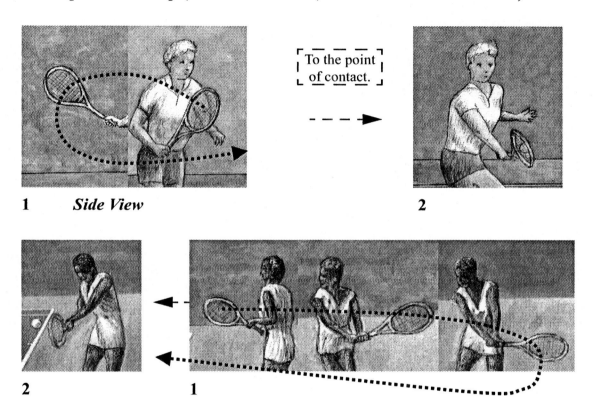

1   *Side View*   To the point of contact.   2

2   1

• **Extended "C" Loop**

Great racquet head acceleration due to high racquet head backswing.

To the point of contact.

Ball level

1

2   *Side View*

• Swing under the level of the coming ball for good topspin production (see "Spins" in Chapter 1).

[1] See *Ready Position* in Chapter 1, **"Stances"**

ANTICIPATION & FOOTWORK

ANTICIPATION & FOOTWORK

Realizing where your opponent intends to aim his next shot is a big weapon against his strategy. Anticipation will neutralize his attack (keeping the ball in play effectively)[1] and might force him into a defensive plan, shifting the percentage to your side (offensive or attacking game has a higher percentage rate of success than defensive game).[2]

Anticipation is a matter of:
1. Recovering to the "Recovery Site."
2. Watching the opponent's racquet face (reacting quicker).
3. Understanding the next possible shot.
4. Footwork. Getting to the ball early.

Also consider:
- Understanding the effects of spin.[3]
- Opponent's pattern of play (especially under pressure).

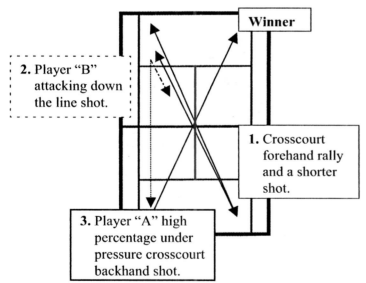

2. Player "B" attacking down the line shot.

Winner

1. Crosscourt forehand rally and a shorter shot.

3. Player "A" high percentage under pressure crosscourt backhand shot.

In the example shown to the left, there are two patterns of play. Player "A" keeps the ball crosscourt, rallying patiently (high percentage), and Player "B" hits a more aggressive shot without realizing that his opponent reacts under pressure with another crosscourt shot (automatically). As in any other case, every player should be ready for any shot, but having a feel for a possible next shot (anticipation), will quicken your reaction time and, this way, you will reach the ball sooner.

Some players have a tendency to have specific patterns of rallies and a particular shot when under pressure. Recognizing those shots and patterns of play will help you anticipate your opponent's next shot and, therefore, control the point.
- Sound of opponent's shot (brush for spin).
- Speed and height of the ball.

1. RECOVERING (and Covering the Court)

Your position in the court depends on your executed shot. For this reason, after every shot you will need to know where is the best place on the court to position yourself (recovering) so you can reach any shot by your opponent.

Because you need to cover only a few yards (from center of the court), you might think that with just speed and acceleration it is possible to cover the whole court well, but:

- Recovering to the "**Recovery Site**" will make your speed become secondary, and will help you to cover the court easily and effectively. By recovering to the correct spot you will save steps, and, therefore, your tactical plan will become primary (getting to the ball early and hitting the chosen shot).

- Speed and acceleration (as well as quickness of the first step) still are indispensable ingredients for good coverage of the court.

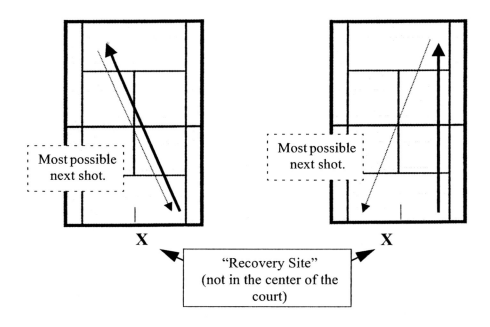

Most possible next shot.

Most possible next shot.

X   X

"Recovery Site"
(not in the center of the court)

• The **"Recovery Site"** depends on the executed shot.

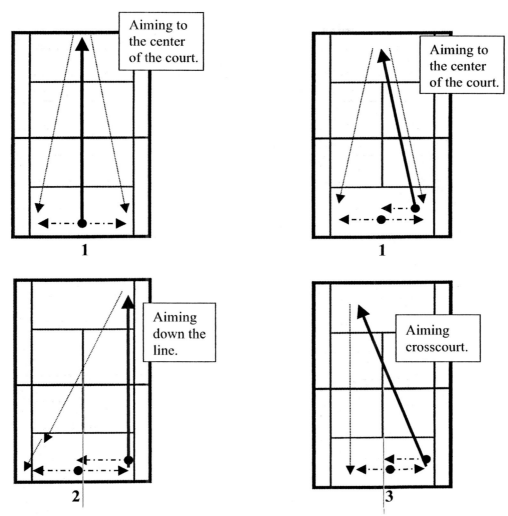

The "Recovery Site" is located in the center of reach for any possible opponent's shot.

• Recover to site **1** (center) after a straight shot to the center of the court to reach the best possible return.

• Recover to site **2** (left from center) after a down-the-line shot to reach the best possible return.

• Recover to site **3** (right from center) after a crosscourt shot to reach the best possible return.

HOW TO RECOVER

For a quick and efficient recovery, the back foot on every square and closed stance shot steps to the *outside* and pushes off to shuffle to the "Recovery Site," or cross steps to run to the next shot.

Push off from outside foot to recover.

1   **2**

The back foot steps out to stop the body inertia and pushes off to recover.

1   **2**

Open stance players are ready to push off from the outside foot.

Recover.

1   **2**   **3**

Shuffle when the "Recovery Site" is not far away, as in a crosscourt rally.

Cross step when you are far from the "Recovery Site" and a quick recovery is necessary.

2. WATCHING THE OPPONENT'S RACQUET FACE

As the split step is in progress (feet off the ground), your eyes should be on the opponent's racquet face as he strikes the ball. This action will provide your brain with enough information, as you land on the ground, to start moving early (or at least reacting) toward the opponent's intended target area as well as helping you to read speed, spin, and height of the shot (i.e. an open racquet face signals a lob).

As the opponent's ball crosses the net, you should be already in position to hit the shot (early preparation) at opponent's target area, waiting for the ball to bounce on your side.

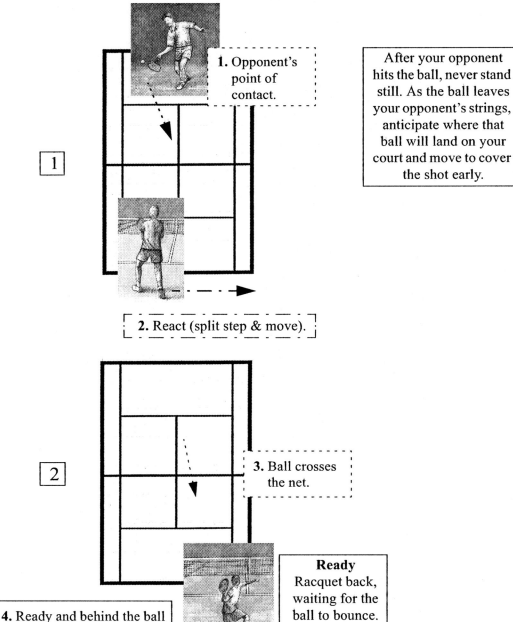

1. Opponent's point of contact.

After your opponent hits the ball, never stand still. As the ball leaves your opponent's strings, anticipate where that ball will land on your court and move to cover the shot early.

2. React (split step & move).

3. Ball crosses the net.

Ready
Racquet back, waiting for the ball to bounce.

4. Ready and behind the ball before the ball bounces.

• Also, be aware of your opponent's position on the court (next possible shot), clues from his grip, stance, backswing, and the position of the toss when serving.

3. UNDERSTANDING THE NEXT POSSIBLE SHOT

Understanding the next possible shot will not only help you get to the ball early, but it will let you play on "automatic pilot," which, consequently, will lead you to play in "the zone." Playing in "the zone" is an expression that professional players use when they are playing in a comfort zone (perfect points of contact), where every shot works, footwork is quick and agile (light-footed), and an overall good feel is perceived. Note that all the examples can be reversed.

- When you are attacking with a deep corner shot and moving in to the net, your opponent might get out of trouble with a **lob**.

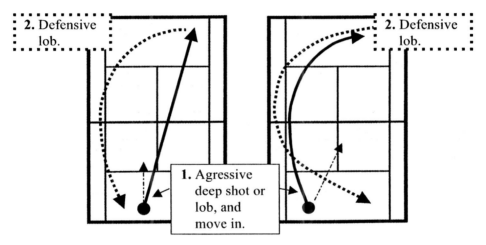

- On a crosscourt rally, the first shorter ball might be a **down-the-line + follow to the net**.

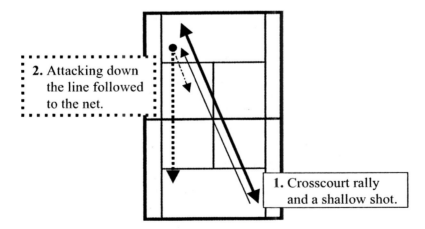

- When you are pushed deep behind the baseline, expect a **drop shot** (especially on slow courts like clay).

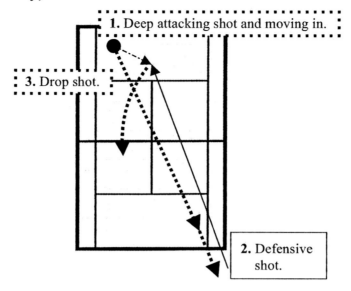

- If your movement is not the best, or you are not recovering well, your opponent might try to move you around the court, going for the **open court**.

- Most of the time, high percentage chance of put-away shots will go to the **open court**.

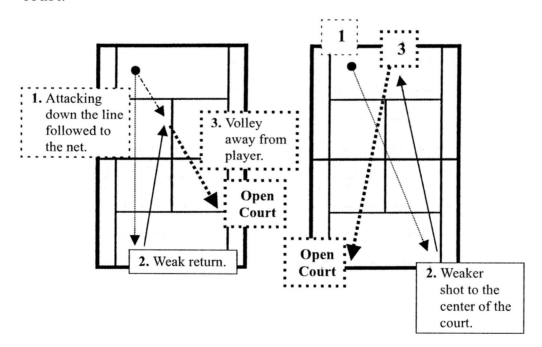

• After hitting a **passing shot** down the line, **move in** diagonally forward as though following the ball, cutting off the angle, covering any possible opponent's volley (usually if the passing shot is a **forcing shot**, your opponent will return a weak, short volley or fall into an "under pressure" pattern of play).

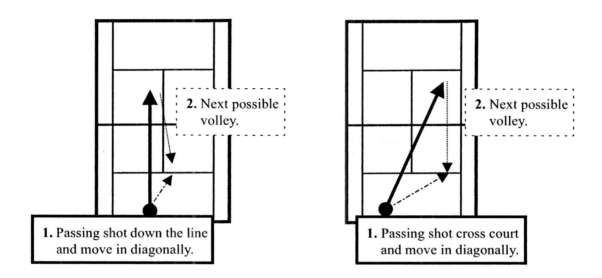

2. Next possible volley.

2. Next possible volley.

1. Passing shot down the line and move in diagonally.

1. Passing shot cross court and move in diagonally.

• When hitting a **drop shot, move in** to cover your opponent's drop shot or angle shot return.

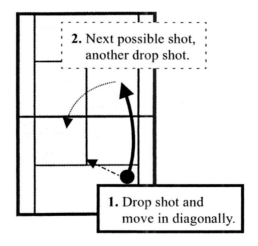

2. Next possible shot, another drop shot.

1. Drop shot and move in diagonally.

* Also consider what your opponent might ***not do*** on each particular situation (cutting off possibilities).

4. FOOTWORK

Footwork is a major factor for success in practically every sport, but in tennis, high-performance footwork is particularly essential. Tennis is a game of constant emergencies, where every shot can be hit at different speeds, spins, heights, and placements. Therefore, being agile and quick (as well as being able to keep dynamic balance) is a must in order to do all the sorts of specific steps and movements required to reach the ball early.

How do the pros make it look so easy to run and get to every ball? How do they manage to be always in the right place at the right time? The answer is that they anticipate the next shot, and they are never flat-footed while the point is in play. They maintain constant movement: split step/react, get to the ball, recover.

A. SPLIT STEP / REACT

KEYS:
Timing / Eye on the ball
Balance
Quick reaction (quick decision-making and quick reaction speed)

- Split step builds a foundation to react to the next ball, taking yourself from a balanced position to a spring-like position. This reaction should follow with an explosive first step. It starts as a little hop in the air. It should be done every time during the point, just **before** your opponent's racquet makes contact with the ball.

Lean forward with the racquet ready out in front.

1

2

Feet shoulder width apart.

• The **timing** is the most important ingredient of the split step. When the ball is struck on your opponent's strings, you should be off the ground **(1)**. As you land on the ground **(2)**, your body stores energy (and gets into a balanced position) and so you can move quickly in any direction, according to your opponent's shot (including moving back for overheads and forward for volleys).

Note: Make sure that the split step is not done after the ball leaves the opponent's strings. That is why it is recommended you do the split just before your opponent's actual point of contact.

• As you land, you should not fall on both feet at the same time. It is more effective to land with the opposite foot first for the desired shot. For example, for a forehand a right handed player should land first with the left toes, so the foot will push off, facilitating and preparing the shoulder rotation for the coming shot (first thing right after the split step), and vice versa for the backhand.

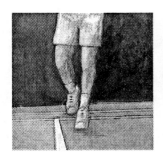 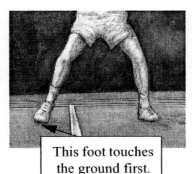 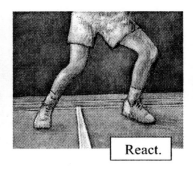

This foot touches the ground first.

React.

Using a split step also helps you keep your eyes on the ball, especially at the opponent's point of contact, maximizing your anticipation (as well as helping you keep good rhythm with the ball) and balance, and therefore helps you move well.

• You do not have to be on the balls of your feet all the time, but an efficient split step starts and finishes on the toes.

Remember: The reason you split is to get to the next shot more quickly, so don't split and stay ——► **split and react** (move).

B. GETTING TO THE BALL

GROUNDSTROKES

If the ball is short, attack by moving forward quickly and hitting the ball off your front foot. For a more aggressive shot, advanced players can jump off the front foot (dynamic balance must be maintained), falling on the same front foot and continuing to move forward.

Jump off the front foot.

Fall on the front foot and move forward.

1   2   3

If the ball is deep into the court and behind you, hit a defensive shot off your back foot but transfer your weight to your front foot. For a more aggressive defensive shot, advanced players can jump off the back foot (dynamic balance must be maintained), landing on the same back foot, and then transferring the weight forward to the front foot (usually forehands).

Open stance.

Jump off the back foot.

1. Early Preparation   **2. Point of Contact**

3. Follow Through   4. Recovery

If the ball is close to you, a side step shuffle is the most effective movement, because once you get to the ball you will be ready to hit an open stance shot, or a square shot if you step forward. After shuffling, your shoulders must turn accordingly (forehand or backhand). Shuffling also is an easy and natural movement that allows you to watch your opponent (especially at his point of contact) as you move toward the ball or recovery.

On clay courts, there is always some degree of sliding. If you play with a square stance, instead of stepping forward as you would do on hard courts, slide the front foot, thereby creating a more stable stance. Also, on groundstrokes, as you get close to the ball, always make little adjustment steps to fine tune the distance between you and the ball in order to have a consistent point of contact.

If the ball is far from you, right after the split step **(1)**, first turn your shoulders accordingly by loading weight onto the outside foot or the side you are running to **(2)**, and simultaneously slide that foot towards the center of your body weight (Drop Step).

Split Step   Drop Step   Cross Step

37

As you get sideways, using a cross step, run to the ball with wide steps, moving both hands in order to accelerate to the ball **(3)**. Use the racquet to maintain balance as you move the hands. Once you get to the ball, small fine-tuning steps are required to make a perfect point of contact. Eyes must be locked on the ball and head kept steady throughout the shot.

For an explosive forward reaction on clay courts, slide the back foot to set up the front foot (loading the front foot).

Split Step / React   Slide Back Foot   Push Off the Front Foot

An ***inside-out forehand*** is a forehand hit from a backhand position (running around the backhand). It is a very aggressive shot, but requires agile footwork and quick back-pedaling to set the shoulders and get ready to strike the ball. It is usually placed deep in the opponent's backhand corner (right-handed player) or close to the intersection of the singles sideline and the service line to open up the court.

Split Step / React   Back-Pedal   Early Preparation

On clay courts, reaching for a wide ball is more complex than on hard courts. Sliding is a must for the obvious reason that you cannot stop your body's inertia as you can on hard courts. The point of contact should be executed at the end of the slide; otherwise you will get too far from the "Recovery Site."

End of Slide / Point of Contact

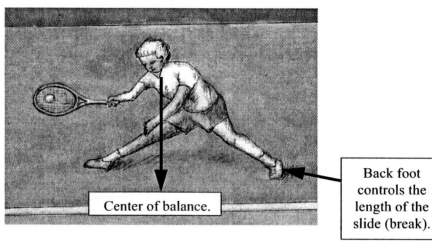

Center of balance.

Back foot controls the length of the slide (break).

Open stance shots create a solid foundation for sliding. Square stances take longer to recover from due to the need for the extra step (back foot steps to the outside). For either stance, in order to slide efficiently, your weight should be distributed evenly at your center of balance, keeping your body fairly low to cover more ground without sacrificing balance. The control factor for the length of the slide is how your weight is transferred onto the back foot. The more weight you place on the back foot, the more you break. If your weight is on the front foot, you won't be able to slide (loss of dynamic balance). It is important to keep the head still throughout the slide so your eyes can stay locked on the ball and you can maintain dynamic balance.

Hitting on Full Run

Ideally, you should work on quick, explosive footwork (especially the very first step) to get to the ball early and have time to stop and hit the ball in balance. Today, top players are very powerful thanks to cross training, proper diet, and racquet technology, so some shots can be hit on full run while still keeping dynamic balance and producing a very aggressive shot (even on closed stances, whenever it is required). Under very hard situations, when power cannot be greatly produced, a lob is a good way out.

Running strokes should be hit off the front foot for many reasons:

Forehand

- On the full run, inertia will carry you one or more steps, so having the point of contact off the front foot, the following step will be with the back foot. This leaves you in a perfect position to get to your "Recovery Site" using the back foot for a cross step. It also helps to stop your body from further running (inertia).

- Hitting off your front foot will transfer most of your potential energy (weight) into the shot. The hips will rotate only with the extra step (back foot steps to the outside), generating some more power and acceleration on the follow-through.

- When the point of contact is late or behind, hitting off the back foot is still very effective on the forehand side (especially aiming down the line) due to the position of the dominant shoulder (right shoulder is behind for a right-handed player).

- Players with open stance forehands will find it much harder to hit the ball and to transfer the weight forward (open stance needs to be closer to the ball compared to a closed or square stance).

Backhand

- One or two-handed backhands are much tougher to hit off the back foot because of the position of the dominant shoulder (right shoulder is in front for a right-handed player). As the ball is struck off the back foot, the weight cannot be transferred forward.

VOLLEY

If the Ball Is Hit Right at You

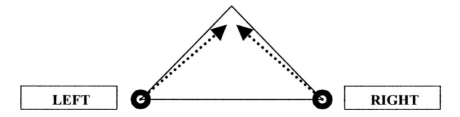

For an aggressive punch volley, step to the apex of the triangle according to the volley (left foot for a right-handed forehand, right foot for a backhand) before making contact.

LEFT   RIGHT

Foot Positioning during a Punch Volley (*Front View*)

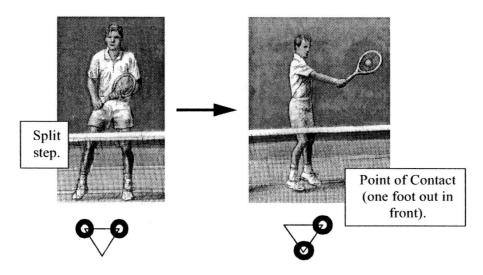

Split step.

Point of Contact (one foot out in front).

If the Ball Is Away

5. Recover with the back foot stepping to the outside.

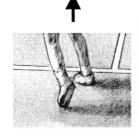

4. Step up in front according to the particular volley. Use a cross step only for shots that are too far to reach or when you are late.

3. Move right after the split with the outside foot towards the intended point of contact, cutting off the angle (Jab Step).

2. SPLIT STEP

1. FOOTWORK

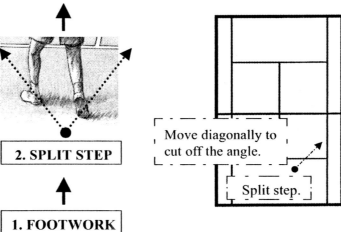

Move diagonally to cut off the angle.

Split step.

If the Ball Is Too Far Away

When a ball is too far from your reach, and good footwork cannot make a difference, the last resort is a stab volley, which most likely will produce a drop volley.[4]

For a quick and effective lunge, after the split step, move first with the outside foot towards the shot (large Jab Step) as you push off with the other foot, and then cross over with it to finally reach the ball or to control your body balance. Racquet face remains as vertical as possible throughout the point of contact. The free hand always helps to control the body balance (forehand and backhand).

Note: **Recovering** footwork patterns and **positioning** (recovering to the "Recovery Site") for all volleys are performed as groundstrokes.[2]

SERVE

There are many footwork options on how to start the serve, and all of them are acceptable. What you choose is a matter of preference, and, eventually, if it is consistent, it will become part of your style. The most common footwork patterns are:

Pushing off the front foot and landing with it inside the court, following with the back (right) foot forward, getting ready to do a split step or to keep running forward for a "serve & volley" game.

- Simple and effective for all game styles.
- Excellent for "serve & volley" type of game (easy to get well inside the court, therefore, easy to reach the net) or for aggressive serves (good angular and forward momentum production).

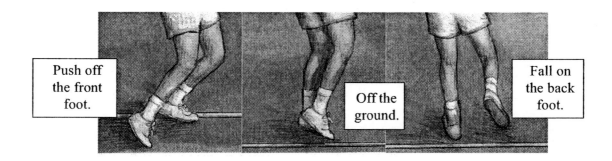

Push off the front foot.

Off the ground.

Fall on the back foot.

Pushing off the front foot and landing with the back foot first inside the court, following with the left, getting ready to do a split step.

- Good angular (trunk) rotation.
- Effective if staying back for baseline type of game.

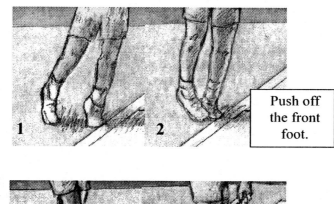

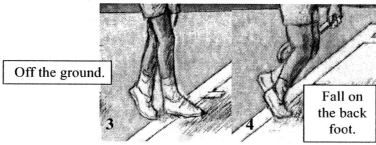

Dragging the back foot to the back of the front foot and pushing off from the front foot, landing first with the front foot inside the court, and following with the back (right) foot forward, getting ready to do a split step or to continue to run forward for a "serve & volley" game.

- Excellent spin production thanks to both feet aggressively pushing upward in synch with the arm.
- Excellent for "serve & volley" type of game. Not only can it create aggressive topspin, but by falling on the front foot well inside the court followed by the back (right) foot, you can also create angular and forward momentum, which, consequently, allows you to reach the net quickly.
- The only drawback is lack of balance due to the small base formed when the back foot is dragged to the back of the front foot.

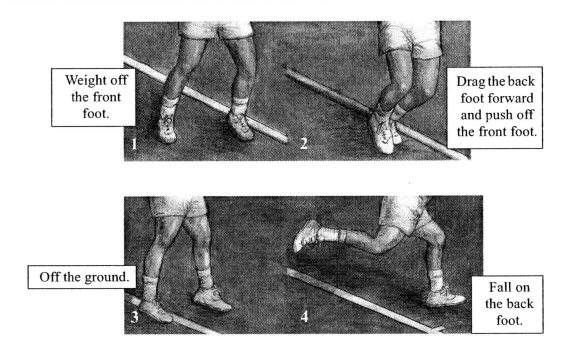

Weight off the front foot.

Drag the back foot forward and push off the front foot.

Off the ground.

Fall on the back foot.

RETURN OF SERVE

Although the return of serve is a completely different stroke from the volley, the footwork patterns are similar.

A

1. Split step.

2. **If the ball is right at you,** load the outside foot as you set the racquet.

3. Step up in front and make contact.

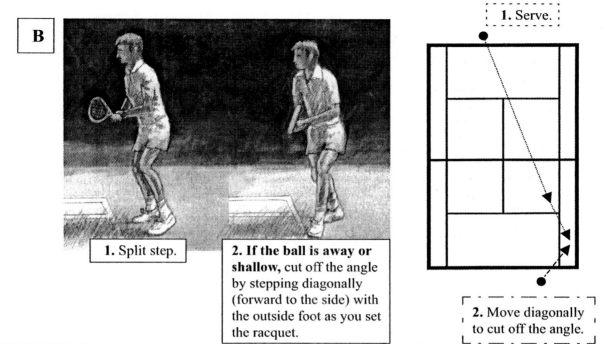

B

1. Serve.

1. Split step.

2. **If the ball is away or shallow,** cut off the angle by stepping diagonally (forward to the side) with the outside foot as you set the racquet.

2. Move diagonally to cut off the angle.

OVERHEAD

HOW TO MOVE BACK

- By stepping back with the right foot (the same foot that holds the racquet) right after the split step, not only are you getting away from the net more quickly, but because you are turned sideways you are also setting up for quick, back-stepping footwork.

Back foot steps back.   Front foot pushes back.

- Once you are faced sideways, use side step shuffles or cross steps to move back.

Cross Step

- If the ball is still too high by the time you need to make contact, use a scissors-kick jump or a straight-up jump. The straight-up jump is more often used with the side step shuffle, and it is hard to maintain dynamic balance throughout the stroke (no angular rotation and difficult to transfer the weight forward).

Scissors Kick Jump

Back foot.

Jump off the back foot.

Fall on the front foot.

APPROACH SHOT

Because you need to get to the ball at the maximum height of its bounce, and so you can reach the net as early as possible to cut down on the reaction time of your opponent, footwork efficiency is the most important ingredient factor for a good approach shot.

JUMPING OFF THE FRONT FOOT[5]

• Very aggressive approach shots.

• Best for topspin shots and two-handed backhands.

CARRIOCA STEP

• Best for one hand backhand slice shots.

• The carrioca step (back foot steps ***behind*** front foot) happens right ***after*** the point of contact, allowing the hips to stay sideways throughout the slice stroke on the one hand backhand, and therefore allowing you to hit through the shot (without completely stopping), imparting good underspin with accuracy.

- On the one-handed backhand slice, do the carrioca step *after* the point of contact (as follow through is performed).

- On the forehand slice and the two-handed backhand (slice and topspin), the back foot steps in *front* of the front foot. This step happens *before* the point of contact, helping you move through and move quicker towards the net.

RUNNING DOWN A LOB

1. EARLY RECOGNITION

- Right after the split step, recognize that is a lob (unreachable overhead smash).

Use a back step to turn.

1. Split Step   **2. React**

2. TURN AND RUN

- Quickly turn backward using a **back step** (same foot that holds the racquet) for the lobs directed over your head or over the forehand side of your body, and run the lob down along the side of the ball (not right under it) while still watching the ball. If the ball goes over the backhand side, just turn around and run the ball down.
- Run quicker than the flight of ball in order to get behind it (beat the ball).
- Always run back a step more than necessary because is much easier to adjust forward on the last split second than to hit it late.

Watch the ball while running.

Run on either side of the ball to get in position to hit it.

3. POINT OF CONTACT

- Hit the ball accordingly (depending on which side of the ball you are on), rotating your body 180 degrees (facing forward to the net), pivoting on the back foot (forehand and backhand).
- Racquet face should be slightly open to hit back a deep lob.[6, 7]

Pivot off the back foot.

Point of Contact

4. FOLLOW THROUGH

- Follow through as body keeps rotating.
- Weight should be transferred to the front foot.
- Finish high in order to get good height and depth.

5. RECOVERY

Back foot steps
to the outside.

DROP SHOT

Do not hit the drop shot at a full run. Before point of contact, slow down your speed, as the arm, wrist, and racquet absorb most of the energy to produce an effective drop shot. On clay courts, contact the ball at the end of the slide.

[1] See *Groundstroke Strategy* in Chapter 5, **"Groundstroke Strategy"**
[2] See *Different Players* in Chapter 5, **"Different Players"**
[3] See *Spins* in Chapter 1, **"Spins"**
[4] See *Volley* in Chapter 2, **"Volleys"**
[5] See *If the Ball is Short* in Chapter 1, **"Anticipation & Footwork"**
[6] See *Lob* in Chapter 4, **"Lob"**
[7] See *Lob Strategy* in Chapter 5, **"Lob Strategy"**

<u>SPINS</u>

MAXIMIZING CONTROL: <u>SPINS</u>

Spin can be used for a number of reasons. By utilizing topspin, some players can be more aggressive. Others, like retrievers, use more defensive tactics, exploiting the underspin. But there is more than that when the ball spins. The ball rotation can tell you how the ball is going to bounce when it touches the ground. The amount of revolutions on the ball also can tell you about its flight and depth (together with the speed and height of your opponent's shot). You can anticipate the shot better if you understand the spin as it flies to your side and, therefore, you can be better prepared for the next shot.

Also, a combination of heavy spin (topspin), power and mass (your body and racquet weight transferred into the ball at striking time) creates a heavy ball. This kind of shot is an advanced shot, much harder to return than a flat or light-spanned shot.

So, if spin controls the flight of the ball, and you control spin, you control the point.

STROKES

TOPSPIN *(Side View)*

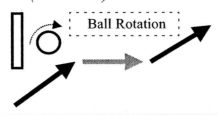

Ball Rotation

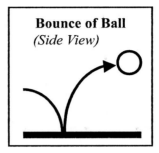

Bounce of Ball
(Side View)

Energy Vectors
Racquet face should follow the direction of the vectors, brushing the backside of the ball, *low to high*, without changing its angle. The more upward the black vectors (and faster the acceleration), the more pronounced the spin created (as with a topspin lob).

Effect of Spin:

- Increases air pressure on top of the ball, causing the ball to drop quickly.
- Ball rebounds off the court surface quicker, higher, and farther (kicks up) than a flat shot.

Benefits:

- A shot with extreme topspin can kick over the head level, making a tough shot to return, as well as keeping your opponent deep.
- Aggressive shot that can force your opponent to return weakly.
- Easy to clear the net, as the ball tends to stay in the court.

Playing against a Topspinner:

- The opponent's topspin shot will push you to the back of the court, so make sure that your shots *do not get short*; return deep with pace; otherwise, your opponent will attack your shallow shots.
- Try to take the ball on the rise. This way, you can stay close or inside the baseline and maintain your offense.
- Be aware of how spin affects the bounce of the ball (angle of incidence). If the opponent's shots land short (2-3 feet behind the service line) but with heavy topspin, those shots can still push you back well behind the baseline.

UNDERSPIN — SLICE *(Side View)*

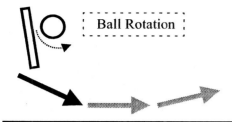

Ball Rotation

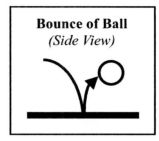

Bounce of Ball
(Side View)

> ***Energy Vectors***
> Racquet face should follow the direction of
> the vectors, brushing the backside of the
> ball, *high to low* and through, without
> changing its angle. The more downward the
> black vector (and faster the acceleration),
> the more pronounced the spin created.

Effect of spin:

- Increases air pressure under the ball, causing the ball to float.
- Ball rebounds off the court surface slower, lower, and straighter up (sits) than a flat shot.

Benefits:

- Natural backhand motion. Low energy expenditure thanks to gravity.
- Keeps the bounce of the volleys *low*, forcing the opponent to hit *up*.
- Use on drop shots, floaters, and defensive game (backhand slice, lobs).

Playing against an Underspinner:

- Because the underspin rotation of your opponent's shot as it comes to you has the same rotation of your topspin, be careful (hit through the ball, making a solid contact) and lift the ball well, otherwise it might end up in the net.

Opponent's Underspin → **Your Topspin** → **Same Rotation**

- Be aware of how spin affects the bounce of the ball. You will need to get closer than normal to the bounce of a ball hit with heavy underspin because that shot will "sit up" and stay low.

SIDESPIN *(Back View)*

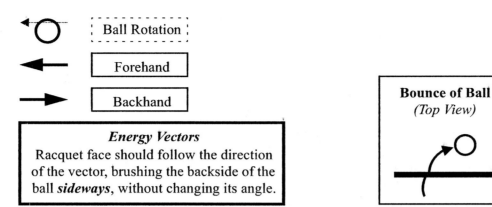

Ball Rotation

Forehand

Backhand

Energy Vectors
Racquet face should follow the direction of the vector, brushing the backside of the ball *sideways*, without changing its angle.

Bounce of Ball
(Top View)

Effect of Spin:

- Increases air pressure on the outside of ball, causing the ball to shift (curve) right or left according to the brush.
- Ball rebounds off the court surface with a pronounced side curve.

Benefits:

- Opens up the court.
- Jams or gets away from opponent. When hitting a sidespin forehand to your opponent's right (forehand), you can jam the player, and when hitting to his left (backhand), the ball gets away from him (same principles apply when hitting sidespin backhands).
- Effective use for inside out forehands.

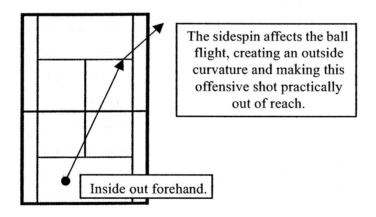

The sidespin affects the ball flight, creating an outside curvature and making this offensive shot practically out of reach.

Inside out forehand.

FLAT *(Side View)*

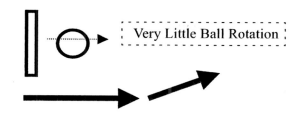

Very Little Ball Rotation

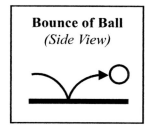

Bounce of Ball
(Side View)

Energy Vectors
Racquet face should follow the direction of the vectors, hitting the backside of the ball ***straight on***, without brushing or changing its angle (some topspin creation).

Effect of Spin:

- Even though the ball is hit flat, there is always a small amount of spin on the ball.
- There is little or no effect on the angle of incidence after the bounce of the ball.

Benefits:

- Quick, sharp, and aggressive shots.
- Good to put away short and high shots (well over the net level).

SERVE

TOPSPIN *(Back View)*

Ball Rotation

Energy Vectors
Racquet face should follow the direction of the vector (gray arrow), extending upward with the body and arm, and brushing the backside of the ball *7 to 1* (black arrow) with the wrist. After contact, the wrist snaps and racquet follows straight forward (hollow arrow) to the target.

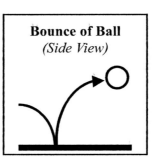

Bounce of Ball
(Side View)

Recommended Grips:[1]

- Eastern backhand.
- Continental.
- Semi-Western backhand.

Toss Placement:

- Over the head (the back arches backwards to produce good topspin).

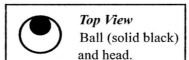

Top View
Ball (solid black) and head.

Most Effective:

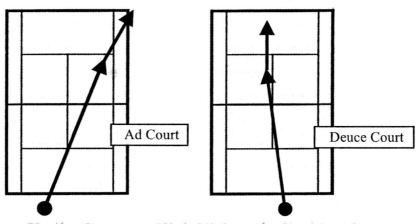

Ad Court

Deuce Court

Open Up the Court   **High Kick to the Backhand**

<u>SLICE</u> *(Back View)*

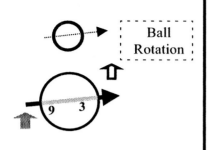

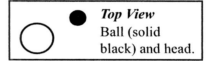

Energy Vectors
Racquet face should follow the direction of the vector (gray arrow), extending upward with the body and arm, and brushing the backside of the ball *9 to 3* (black arrow) with the wrist. After contact, the wrist snaps and racquet follows straight forward (hollow arrow) to the target.

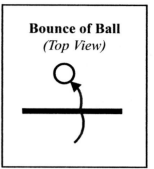

Bounce of Ball
(Top View)

Recommended Grips:[1]
- Eastern backhand.
- Continental.

Toss Placement:
- Out in front to the right.

Top View
Ball (solid black) and head.

Most Effective:

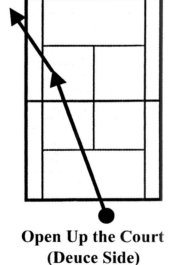

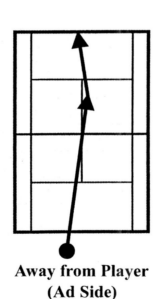

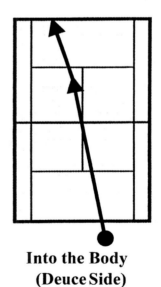

**Open Up the Court
(Deuce Side)**   **Away from Player
(Ad Side)**   **Into the Body
(Deuce Side)**

61

MIX *(Back View)*

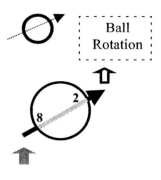

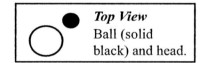

Ball Rotation

Energy Vectors
Racquet face should follow the direction of the vector (gray arrow), extending upward with the body and arm, and brushing the backside of the ball *8 to 2* (black arrow) with the wrist. After contact, the wrist snaps and racquet follows straight forward (hollow arrow) to the target.

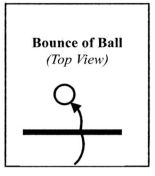

Bounce of Ball
(Top View)

Recommended Grips:[1]

- Eastern backhand.
- Continental.

Toss Placement:

- Out in front to the right, but not as far to the right as the slice serve.

Top View
Ball (solid black) and head.

Most Effective:

- The mix serve is a combination of the topspin and the slice. It is easy to produce and very effective in any situation (good amount of spin and power).

FLAT *(Back View)*

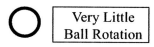

Very Little Ball Rotation

Energy Vectors
Energy Vector (black dot) gets right into the ball. Racquet face should follow the direction of the vector, hitting flat into the ball as the body, arm, and wrist extends upward (gray arrow). After contact, the wrist snaps and racquet follows straight forward (hollow arrow) to the target.

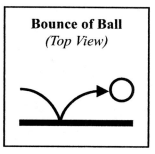

Bounce of Ball
(Top View)

Recommended Grips:[1]

- Continental.
- Eastern forehand (beginners only).

Toss Placement:

- Well out in front and slightly to the right.

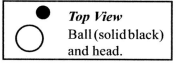

Top View
Ball (solid black) and head.

Most Effective:

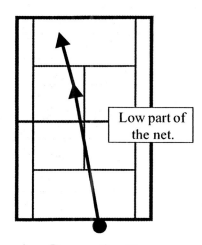

Low part of the net.

Ace Down the T
(Ad and Deuce Court)

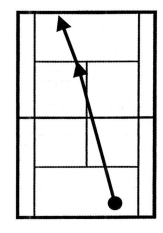

Into the Body
(Ad and Deuce Court)

* In addition to mastering spins, in order to maximize control, use more leg extension and shoulder rotation, and less arm and wrist movements. When joints of the playing arm and wrist are used with excess of motion (or too loosely), especially at point of contact, control will be diminished. The wrist is a good source of power and spin, but it must be used in moderation and in a controlled manner.

[1] See Chapter 1, **"Grips"**

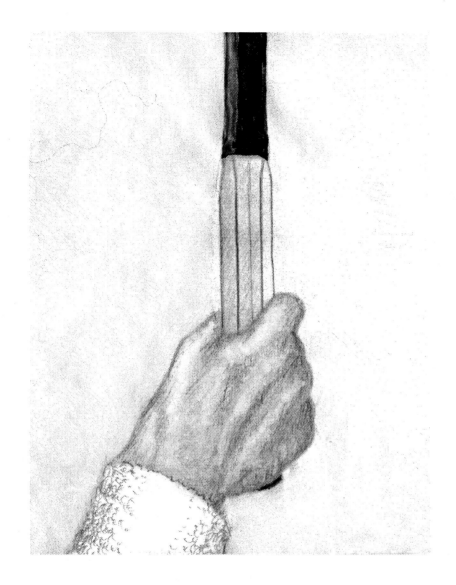

<u>GRIPS</u>

GRIPS

The grip of the racquet is the foundation of all tennis strokes. How you hold the racquet will influence the angle of the racquet face and placement of the point of contact in relation to your body (the striking zone).

Grip selection is flexible and will depend on many factors, such as height of the player (comfort zone), game styles (type of player),[1] and the intention of placement and spin (tactics). Other factors are height of the bounce and court surface.

Note: All grip references are intended for right-handed players. Lefty players can easily convert these notes by using a mirror view (opposite without changing the specifics).

HOW TO FIND THE GRIPS

1. Locate the diagonal part of your palm from the base knuckle of the index finger, through the center of the palm, to the heel.
2. Place this area on the racquet grip, holding the racquet on edge, according to the illustrations.

Racquet on edge

End cap edges

EASTERN FOREHAND

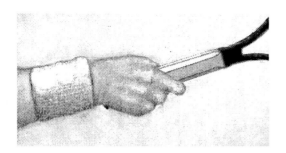

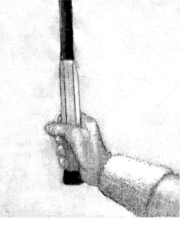

Quick Find:

- Holding the racquet on edge (perpendicular) with the left hand, shake hands with the grip.
- Holding the racquet on edge from its throat, place the right palm flat on the strings and slide it down to the grip.
- "V" formed from the index finger and thumb on edge #2.

Advantages:

- Versatility on all surfaces.
- Easy to generate power.
- Good feel of strength (majority of palm is behind the grip).
- Good topspin development.
- Allows the feel of prolonged ball contact due to vertical racquet face.
- Offers flexibility for different game styles to develop.
- Comfortable striking zone. Point of contact just in front of the front knee at waist level (between mid-trunk and mid-thigh).

Disadvantages:

- Hitting low balls.
- Generating a slice shot without wrist adjustment.
- No spin production if used on serves.

EASTERN BACKHAND

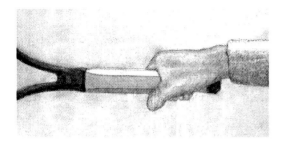

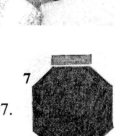

Quick Find:

- Place racquet under the left armpit and grip the racquet with your right hand.
- Hold the racquet on the left side of your body by the pocket, as if it were a sword, and grip the racquet with your right hand.
- "V" formed from the index finger and thumb on edge #7.

Advantages:

- Versatility on all surfaces.
- Good topspin development.
- Allows the feel of prolonged ball contact due to the vertical racquet face.
- Imparts excellent spin on serves (especially for 2nd serve).
- Comfortable striking zone. Point of contact out in front of the front knee at waist level (between mid-trunk and mid-thigh).

Disadvantages:

- Hitting low balls.
- Generating a slice shot without wrist adjustment.
- Weaker than the two-handed backhand (only fingertips behind the grip).
- Need strong forearm muscles to generate a firm shot and spin.

WESTERN FOREHAND

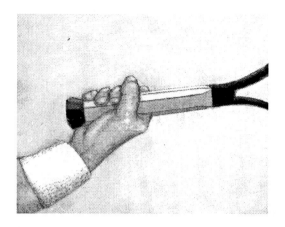

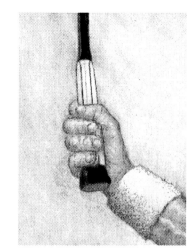

Quick Find:

- Holding the racquet on edge (perpendicular), place your right palm under the grip.
- "V" formed from the index finger and thumb on edge #3.

Advantages:

- Extraordinary topspin (close racquet face on backswing).
- Comfortable high point of contact for high bouncing balls (especially from open stance).[2]

Disadvantages:

- Point of contact must be well out in front of body and above waist level.
- Need for excellent timing.
- Need to flex the wrist (to open the racquet face) on low balls.
- Using the same grip for the backhand puts extreme tension on the elbow and arm, which can lead to tennis elbow.

SEMI-WESTERN FOREHAND

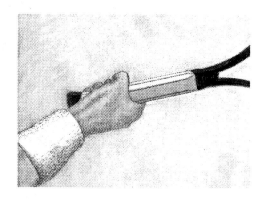 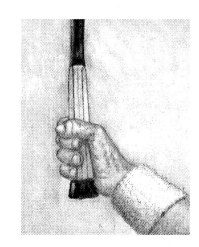

Quick Find:

- In between Eastern and Western forehand grips.
- "V" formed from the index finger and thumb centered on panel #2.

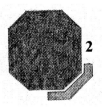

Advantages:

- Imparts good topspin.
- More comfortable than full Western (less stress on the forearm and wrist).
- Point of contact at waist level or above, and out in front of the body.

Disadvantages:

- Difficult for low shots.

SEMI-WESTERN BACKHAND

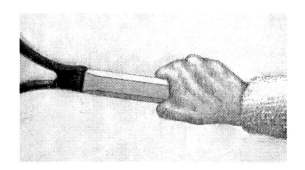
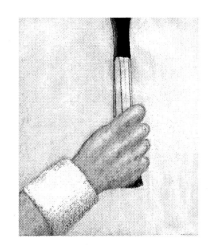

Quick Find:

- Holding the racquet on edge but facing you (parallel to you) at shoulder level, grip the handle right on.
- "V" formed from the index finger and thumb centered on panel #4.

Advantages:

- Excellent topspin production.
- Point of contact at waist level or above, and out in front of the body.

Disadvantages:

- Difficult for low shots.

CONTINENTAL

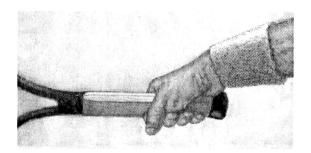

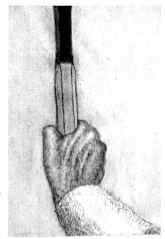

Quick Find:

- Holding the racquet on edge, grip the handle like a hammer.
- Holding the racquet on edge from its throat, place your right palm over the racquet head and slide it all the way down to the grip.
- "V" formed from the index finger and thumb on edge #8.

Advantages:

Point of contact at waist level or below, aligned with the front knee or slightly behind (very little weight transfer).

- Same grip for forehand and backhand.
- Good for low shots.
- Ease on late (slightly behind) and closer-to-the-body shots.
- Excellent for imparting slice (natural open racquet face).
- Easy to impart spin on the serve.
- Easy for quick exchange at the net (volleys).
- Easy for serves, volleys, and overheads (transitional and net game).

Disadvantages:

- Difficult to gain good racquet face control on groundstrokes.
- Except for low balls, all other shots need a strong forearm and wrist.

TWO-HANDED GRIPS

BACKHAND

Though many combinations can be utilized, holding the racquet with the bottom hand (right) in a Continental grip has an advantage over the other combinations. Continental grip is the grip used for the one-hand slice, so in an emergency, a two-handed player can easily release the top hand and slice the shot. Point of contact will vary according to the top hand (left), grip preference, and height of striking zone (comfort zone).

Advantages:
- Increased power.
- Advantage on late point of contacts (slightly behind).
- More acute spin and angles generated by the wrists.
- Better support for manipulating the racquet.
- Restraint from excess rotation, which could lead to tennis elbow.

Disadvantages:
- Shorter reach.
- Difficulty on balls close to the body.
- Needs quicker and more precise footwork.
- Requires good upper body flexibility.
- Difficulty on low balls.

1. EASTERN FOREHAND (Top Left Hand)
EASTERN FOREHAND (Bottom Right Hand)

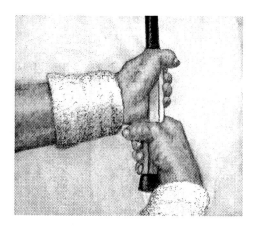

- Good for beginners (quick grip when switching forehand to backhand and vice versa).
- Good support from the top hand, but difficult to control the racquet face due to the wrist position of the bottom hand.
- Hard to produce underspin (slice) due to the bottom hand grip.

2. SEMI-WESTERN FOREHAND (Top Left Hand)
EASTERN FOREHAND (Bottom Right Hand)

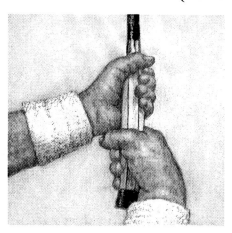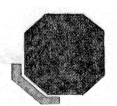

- Same pros and cons of the previous grip (Semi-Western/Eastern forehand).
- Easy on high shots but difficult on low shots due to the top hand grip.

3. EASTERN FOREHAND (Top Left Hand)
CONTINENTAL (Bottom Right Hand)

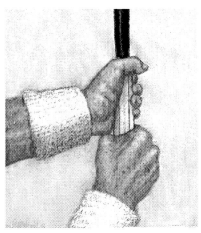

- Versatile grip commonly used by most top professionals.

- Excellent support from the top hand and good racquet face control thanks to the wrist position of the bottom hand.

- Easy to produce underspin shots by releasing the top hand (slice backhand, volleys, drop shots, defensive lobs, as well as stretched emergency shots).

4. SEMI-WESTERN FOREHAND (Top Left Hand)
CONTINENTAL (Bottom Right Hand)

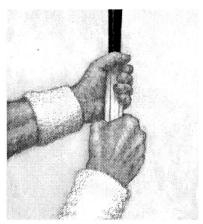

- Same qualities as previous grip (Eastern forehand/Continental) plus pronounced topspin production due to the top hand grip.

Variation

WESTERN FOREHAND (Top Left Hand)
CONTINENTAL (Bottom Right Hand)

• Similar to the previous grip (Semi-Western forehand/Continental) but tougher on low shots.

5. SEMI-WESTERN FOREHAND (Top Left Hand)
EASTERN BACKHAND (Bottom Right Hand)

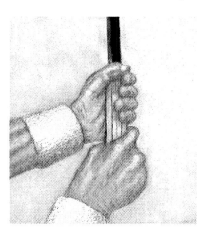 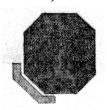 

• Excellent topspin production due to the combination of grips, but limited under-spin shots.

Variation

EASTERN FOREHAND (Top Left Hand)
EASTERN BACKHAND (Bottom Right Hand)

• Similar to previous grip (Semi-Western forehand/Eastern backhand) but tougher on high shots.

FOREHAND

Though not many top players would use a two-handed forehand because of the lack of reach, it is still a powerful, versatile shot. Weak players as well as ambidextrous players can benefit from this shot. Grips are as variable as the two-handed backhand and should be chosen according to preference and height of striking zone. Also, some players change hands when switching from forehand to backhand (top and bottom hands), but some will hold the same grip as the backhand (no switch).

Advantages:
- Powerful.
- Deceiving.
- Good spin production.

Disadvantages:
- Need for extremely quick footwork.
- Requires great upper trunk flexibility.
- Need for excellent fitness.
- If you switch hands from forehand to backhand, it can slow down the preparation face of the stroke, and if you do not switch hands, your hands get crisscrossed, making it a difficult shot to control.

HOW TO CHANGE GRIPS WHILE PLAYING

The change of grips during the point is done automatically with the free hand (the left hand for right-handed players), as the shoulders turn to prepare for the shot. The variation is when time is limited, like when moving to the net (to volley) and returning a serve. The change of grip is done as soon as you realize what shot you are getting (forehand side or backhand) as you split step.[3]

Using one grip, the Continental, for the net game (volleys, overhead, serve & volley game, etc.) is an advantage. Even though there is enough time to make grip changes, the Continental will maintain good wrist position for volleys and apply the necessary spin for serves and overheads, as well as help you to concentrate on the stroke.

[1] See Chapter 5, **"Different Players"**
[2] See Chapter 1, **"Stances"**
[3] See *Split Step* in Chapter 1, **"Anticipation & Footwork"**

CHAPTER 2

BASIC STROKES

FOREHAND

FOREHAND

The Big Weapon

By nature, the forehand is a very powerful shot because most of the palm of the dominant hand is behind the grip. Since the forehand is the most frequently used stroke in a rally, it is commonly developed into a weapon to control the point and to win points.

Also, an aggressive attacker should use the forehand to open up the court or to set up a volley. Players like Jim Courier use the forehand for most shots by running around the backhand, hitting an inside-out crosscourt forehand, and forcing the opponent to hit a low percentage down the line.

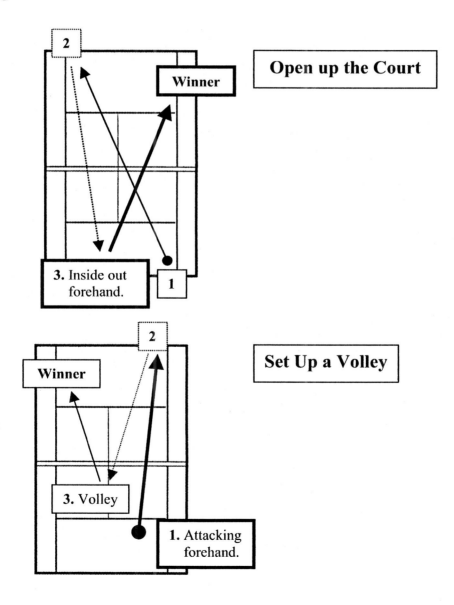

TOPSPIN FOREHAND *FRONT VIEW*

1. Split Step / React   **2. Footwork**

3. Early Preparation   **4. Stop and Step**

5. Point of Contact   **6. Follow Through**   **7. Recovery**

TOPSPIN FOREHAND *SIDE VIEW*

1. Split Step / React   2. Footwork   3. Early Preparation

4. Stop and Step

5. Point of Contact   6. Follow Through   7. Recovery

FOREHAND
TOPSPIN

Square Stance

KEYS:
Early Preparation
Balance
Timing

RECOMMENDED GRIPS:
Eastern, Semi-Western, Western forehand.[1]

1. **SPLIT STEP / REACT**
   - Get ready.[2]

2. **FOOTWORK**
   - Get to the ball early.[2]

Explosive first step.

3. **GOOD EARLY PREPARATION**
   A. Shoulder Turn
   - Turn the shoulders facing sideways (some players turn the shoulders leading with the elbow, and some even lift it, as the racquet is taken back. That's OK but not necessary).
   - Hips turn as well.
   - Chin should almost touch the *front* shoulder to ensure good trunk rotation.
   - Racquet end cap points forward, lining up with the incoming ball (and so the racquet head points back).[3]

- Arm relaxed.
- Wrist relaxed (loose grip).

Racquet goes
back well before
the ball bounces
(as the ball
crosses the net).

- Free hand stretches out in front (to maintain good balance).

B. Weight
- As a rule of thumb, your body weight should be where the racquet head is. In other words, when the racquet is taken *back*, your weight should be on your *back* foot. This is necessary because as the racquet goes forward to the point of contact, your weight (free energy) will transfer to the front foot, transferring all that energy into the shot (even in open stance shots).

C. Knees Bend
- As the racquet is taken back, your knees should be bent down as low as if you were sitting on a chair.

4. STOP AND STEP OUT IN FRONT
A. Stop and Step
- Stop to hit a controlled, balanced shot and step out in front, *toward* the target and not across, as in a closed stance. This effectively transfers the energy of your body links into the ball and toward the intended target.[4]

B. Sideways
- Body stays sideways while body motion stops, maintaining good balance.

C. Head Control
- The head should not move throughout the shot, especially at point of contact. The head is the center of balance of the body; by keeping it still, balance is maintained.

D. Eye Control
- Eyes should be locked on the ball. Watching the ball is an imperative tool for every player. This process starts by watching the opponent's racquet face at point of contact and continues by following the ball to your own bounce and point of contact. Then, without losing track of the ball, continue to follow the ball back to your opponent's racquet. This sequence repeats until the point is over.

- At high-speed tennis, when the ball moves too fast, follow the ball with your eyes but focus especially when it gets to the *peak of the bounce* of your and your opponent's shot (the ball stops, before starts to come down). It is easier to visualize it this way.[5]

E. Forward Motion

- First, the knees extend up, starting the kinetic body chain (power production). Then the hips rotate forward, transferring the ground forces into the trunk; subsequently, the shoulders and arm rotate, then the elbow. Lastly, the wrist snaps forward, delivering the final force into the ball (note that elbow extension and wrist flexion occurs after point of contact). This kinetic chain of body links is one smooth, sequenced motion.[6]
- Make sure that the racquet head is lower than the ball before point of contact in order to generate topspin and good clearance over the net.
- Palm and racquet should face down for better topspin production.

- Free hand stretches out in front for balance.
- Relax arm and forearm (looser grip) so maximum acceleration can be attained.
- When more control is required, *stay low*, maintaining good balance (low center of gravity), to produce a solid point of contact (but no ground force production).

5. POINT OF CONTACT

- Eyes locked on the ball.

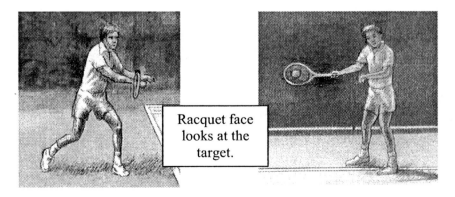

Racquet face looks at the target.

- Racquet is square (face perpendicular to ground and racquet horizontal) and just out in front of the front knee at waist level (comfort zone).
- Elbow close to trunk, controlling the arm swing.
- Shoulders rotate forward, facing the net.
- Wrist firm (firm grip).
- Weight fully transfers to the front foot. Front knee extends. Back foot is on tiptoe, helping to maintain good balance.
- Racquet head achieves maximum acceleration at this point. By no means should the racquet slow down.

6. FOLLOW THROUGH

- Eyes are steady at point of contact (striking zone) for a split second after the ball has left the strings (do not follow the ball with your eyes immediately after the point of contact). This will help to control accuracy of the shot, as well as helping to maintain balance.
- The path of the racquet right after the point of contact is forward toward the target, keeping the face straight, and creating a feel of a longer contact with the ball (like hitting 3 balls continuously, or hitting through the ball), ensuring perfect aim.

- Wrist should be loose to help the racquet create more power (acceleration) and topspin (wrist snap).
- Racquet swings smoothly across the body, finishing high over the shoulder with the knuckles close to the ear (the end cap of the racquet should point forward to the intended target).
- Chin should be close to the right shoulder (ensures full shoulder rotation and good topspin).
- Free hand catches the racquet by the throat or just gets close to it.

A long smooth follow through ensures maximum acceleration at point of contact, and also relaxes the arm and shoulder.

7. RECOVERY

- With the forward momentum of the follow through, the back foot steps outside towards the sideline, pushing the body to shuffle to the "Recovery Site," or cross stepping to run to the next shot. Open stance players have the advantage of having their outside foot ready to push back to the "Recovery Site," saving one step.[2]

FOREHAND VARIATIONS

HIGH FOREHAND

Even though you always should hit the ball at your striking comfort zone (waist level), there will be situations that will be require you to hit at shoulder level, like a high kicking shot or an approach shot.

Follow the basics for any regular forehand, but stress:
- Hitting *through* with topspin, finishing high and over the ball.
- Good use of leg extension (getting a lift off the ground from impulse force).
- Using the back foot for balance on open stances.[2]
- Using the front foot for balance if attacking forward (approach shots).[2]

Note: Most high shots can be hit *off the ground*. Making contact in the air will add more energy (power) to the shot generated from the leg drive (leg muscles) as well as hitting the shot early, all together, a much more offensive shot. Dynamic balance must be maintained throughout the stroke, otherwise, the accuracy will be diminished.

TOPSPIN HIGH FOREHAND *FRONT VIEW*
Open Stance

1. Split Step / React   2. Footwork / 3. Early Preparation

Off the ground.

4. Point of Contact   5. Follow Through

Maintaining dynamic balance.

6. Recovery

FOREHAND
SLICE

The Way Out

The slice forehand is not used as often as the slice backhand, but it is an option. Usually with a forehand, even on late point of contact and hit off the back foot, it is still possible to impart some topspin due to the position of the palm and the shoulder, producing a higher percentage shot (compared to the slice shot).

However, there are a few occasions where the slice forehand is a necessity. The obvious one is the *drop shot*. Another not so common instance is when reaching for the unreachable shot. Sometimes slicing those far wide shots (mostly on clay courts) is the only way to put one more ball over the net and maybe surprise your opponent by returning the impossible shot.

Slice for the approach shots can also be utilized, but most of the time you are better off hitting an aggressive topspin or flat approach shot, forcing your opponent to return a weak shot, giving you an easy time at the net.

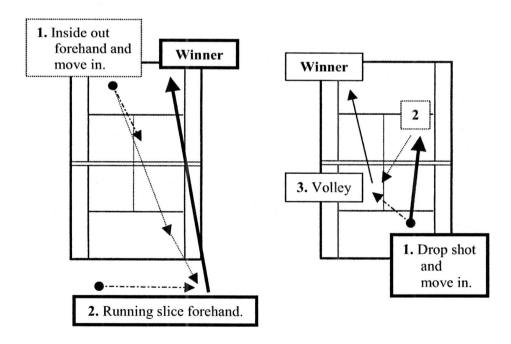

SLIDING SLICE FOREHAND *FRONT VIEW*

3. Early Preparation
(1. Split Step/React / 2. Footwork)

4. Point of Contact

5. Follow Through

SLICE FOREHAND *SIDE VIEW*

2. Footwork   3. Early Preparation
(1. Split Step / React)

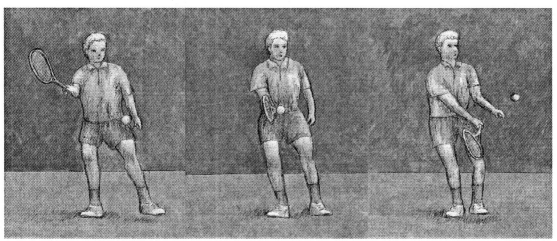

4. Point of Contact   5. Follow Through

6. Recovery

FOREHAND
SLICE

Open Stance

KEYS:
Balance
Timing

RECOMMENDED GRIP:
Continental[1]

1. **SPLIT STEP / REACT**
   - Get ready.[2]

2. **FOOTWORK**
   - Explosive first step.
   - Get to the ball early (drop shots).[2]
   - Get to the ball at full stretch (open stance will help you to reach and disguise those extreme far shots).[2]

3. **EARLY PREPARATION**
   A. Shoulder Turn
   - Turn the shoulders facing sideways.
   - Racquet goes back higher than normal. On defensive running wide shots, the racquet goes just slightly back.
   - Loose wrist.
   B. Weight
   - Weight on back foot in an open stance.[4]
   C. Head Control
   - The head should stay steady throughout the shot to maintain dynamic balance.
   D. Eye Control
   - Eyes should be locked on the ball.[5]
   E. Forward Momentum
   - Racquet swings down and through in a semi-circular motion as you stretch to reach the ball. Make sure that the racquet head is above the incoming ball before point of contact in order to generate underspin.[6] At full stretch, hips and shoulders face forward. Because this shot is an emergency shot, the body kinetic chain is not so effective, and, therefore, ground forces are not maximized.

4. POINT OF CONTACT

- Eyes locked on the ball.
- Racquet face slightly open.
- Ball can be hit at any height (shoulder, waist, or knee level).
- Arm and trunk at full extension (running stretch shot).

- Shoulders facing forward.
- Wrist firm. When underspin is used for a drop shot, loosen up the wrist (loose grip) to absorb the energy of the ball.

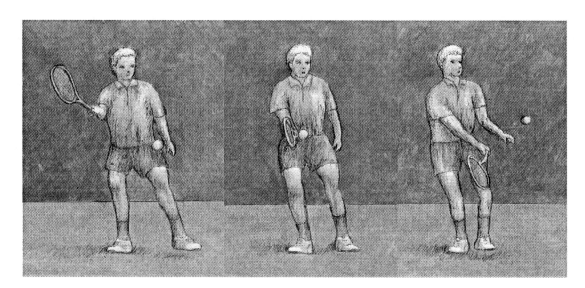

5. FOLLOW THROUGH

- Eyes steady at point of contact (striking zone) for a split second after the ball has left the strings (do not follow the ball with your eyes immediately after point of contact). This will help to control accuracy of the shot, as well as maintain balance.
- Racquet keeps dropping smoothly under the ball and *forward* toward the target, brushing the backside of the ball.[7]
- Palm and racquet open, facing upward, creating depth.
- No weight transfer is possible on wide shots due to the extreme stretch.

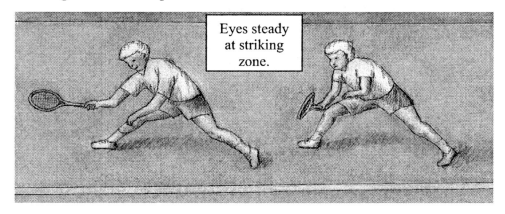

Eyes steady at striking zone.

- Wrist snaps forward (loose wrist) to compensate the lack of weight transfer.
- Free hand helps to control body balance.

6. RECOVERY

- The outside foot pushes the body to shuffle to the "Recovery Site" (or cross step to run to the next shot).[2]

---

[1] See Chapter 1, **"Grips"**
[2] See Chapter 1, **"Anticipation & Footwork"**
[3] See Chapter 1, **"Backswing Styles"**
[4] See Chapter 1, **"Stances"**
[5] See *Focus on the Ball* in Chapter 6, **"While Playing the Match"**
[6] See *Kinetic Body Chain* in Chapter 1, **"Stances"**
[7] See Chapter 1, **"Spins"**

<u>BACKHAND</u>

BACKHAND ONE-HANDED

The "Set Up" Shot

In the last few years, the backhand, like the forehand, has become another weapon shot (topspin backhand). Even though this stroke is one of the most natural motions (the arm and racquet move away from the body), many players choose to develop this stroke as a tool to set up an aggressive attack by opening up the court. For example, a deep crosscourt backhand can leave your opponent on the defensive.

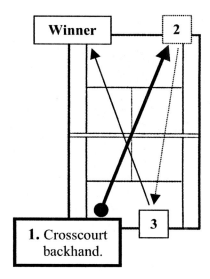

Footwork is the most important ingredient in a precise backhand, especially for the two-handed shot. The most important reason for that is that the shoulder that holds the racquet is out in front, which leaves the player no choice but to hit out in front of the front knee or to hit a weak shot. In contrast, the forehand can be hit a little bit late or behind and still be an aggressive shot (the shoulder that holds the racquet is behind). Therefore, quick footwork and early preparation for good timing are key factors for having an effective and consistent backhand.

ONE-HANDED TOPSPIN BACKHAND *FRONT VIEW*

1. Split Step / React   **2. Footwork**

3. Early Preparation 4. Stop and Step   5. Point of Contact

6. Follow Through   7. Recovery

ONE-HANDED TOPSPIN BACKHAND *SIDE VIEW*

1. Split Step / React   **2. Footwork**

3. Early Preparation   **4. Stop and Step**   **5. Point of Contact**

6. Follow Through   **7. Recovery**

BACKHAND
TWO-HANDED

The Powerful "Set Up" Shot

The two-handed backhand has become the most popular shot at the professional level, especially among women. It is easy to grip and, for that reason, most beginner players choose this stroke (the lack of strength on the dominant arm is also a factor).

Loaded with powerful advantages, this shot can intimidate your opponent and force him into making an error.

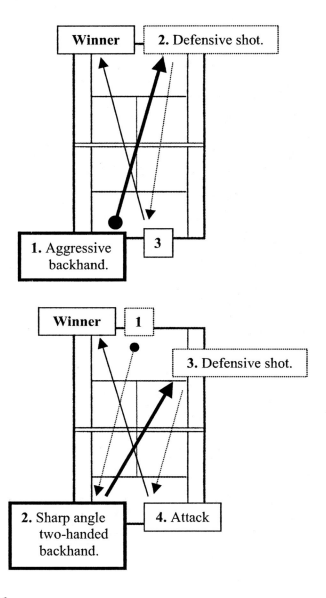

TWO-HANDED TOPSPIN BACKHAND *FRONT VIEW*

1. Split Step/React / 2. Footwork   3. Early Preparation

4. Stop and Step   5. Point of Contact

6. Follow Through   7. Recovery

TWO-HANDED TOPSPIN BACKHAND *SIDE VIEW*

1. Split Step / React   2. Footwork   / 3. Early Preparation

4. Stop and Step   5. Point of Contact

6. Follow Through   7. Recovery

BACKHAND
TOPSPIN

Square Stance

KEYS:
Footwork
Balance
Timing

RECOMMENDED GRIPS:
One-handed backhand: Eastern, Semi-Western backhand.[1]
Two-handed backhand: (bottom/top hand) Continental/Eastern forehand, Continental/Semi-Western forehand, Eastern backhand/Eastern forehand, Eastern backhand/Semi-Western forehand.[1]

1. **SPLIT STEP / REACT**
   - Get ready.[2]

2. **FOOTWORK**
   - Explosive first step.
   - Get to the ball early.[2]

3. **GOOD EARLY PREPARATION**
   A. **Shoulder Turn**
      - Hips turn as well.
      - Chin should almost touch the front shoulder to ensure good trunk rotation.
      - Racquet end cap points forward, lining up with the incoming ball (racquet head points back or just a little more for extra power on one-handed backhands).[3]

Racquet is back well before the ball bounce (as the ball crosses the net).

- Arm relaxed.
- Wrist relaxed (loose grip).
- Free hand holds racquet from the throat and helps to take the racquet back (one-handed backhand).

B. Weight
- As a rule of thumb, your body weight should be where the racquet head is. In other words, when the racquet is taken *back*, your weight should be on your *back* foot. This is necessary because as the racquet goes forward to the point of contact, your weight (free energy) will transfer to the front foot, transferring all that energy into the shot (even from open stances).

C. Knees Bend
- As racquet is taken back, so is your weight. Knees should be bent down as though you were sitting on a chair.

4. STOP AND STEP OUT IN FRONT

A. Stop and Step
- Stop to hit a controlled, balanced shot and step out in front toward the target, trying not to step across the body, as in a closed stance.[4] This effectively transfers the energy of your body links into the ball and toward the intended target.

B. Sideways
- Body stays sideways while body motion stops, maintaining good balance.

C. Head Control
- The head should not move throughout the shot, especially at the point of contact. The head is the center of balance of the body. By keeping it still, you maintain balance.

D. Eye Control
- Eyes should be locked on the ball. Watching the ball is an essential tool for every good player. This process starts by watching the opponent's racquet face and point of contact and continues by following the ball to your own bounce and point of contact. Then, without losing track of the ball, continue to follow the ball back to your opponent's racquet. This sequence repeats until the point is over.
- At high-speed tennis, when the ball moves too fast, follow the ball with your eyes, but focus especially when it gets to the *peak of the bounce* of your and your opponent's shot (when the ball stops before it starts to come down). It is easier to visualize it this way.[5]

E. Forward Motion
- First, the knees extend up, starting the kinetic body chain (power production). Then the hips rotate forward, transferring the ground forces into the trunk. Unlike the two-handed backhand and the forehand, the hips and shoulders in the one-handed backhand do not rotate as much. Subsequently, the shoulders and arm rotate, then the elbow extends, and finally, the wrist snaps forward

(minimally on one-handed backhands), delivering the final force into the ball. This kinetic chain of body links is one smooth, sequenced motion. On the two-handed shot, the sequence of body links does not change, but the hips and shoulder (upper body) rotate forward (facing the net) as the follow through is completed.[6]

- Make sure that the racquet head is lower than the ball before the point of contact in order to generate topspin and get good clearance over the net.
- Relax arm and forearm (looser grip) so maximum acceleration can be attained.
- When more control is required, stay *low*, maintaining good balance (low center of gravity) to produce a solid point of contact (but no ground force production).

5. POINT OF CONTACT
- Eyes locked on the ball.
- Racquet square (face perpendicular to ground and racquet horizontal) and just out in front of the front knee at waist level (comfort zone).

Shoulders and hips rotate forward.

Shoulders and hips stay sideways.

Racquet face looks at the target.

- Dominant arm straight but not locked, elbow in and not leading forward.
- During the *one-handed* shot, the shoulders and hips stay sideways, lining up with the target until the completion of the stroke. On the *two-handed* backhand, the shoulders and hips rotate forward as the racquet completes the follow through.
- Wrist firm.
- Racquet head achieves maximum acceleration at this point. By no means should the racquet slow down.
- Weight fully transfers to front foot. Front knee is extended. Back foot is on tiptoe to help maintain good balance.

6. FOLLOW THROUGH

- Eyes steady at point of contact (striking zone) for a split second after the ball has left the strings (do not follow the ball with your eyes immediately after point of contact). This will help to control accuracy of the shot, as well as maintain balance.

- The path of the racquet right after the point of contact is forward toward the target, keeping the face straight, and creating a feel of a longer contact with the ball (like hitting 3 balls continuously or hitting through the ball), ensuring perfect aiming.
- Racquet swings smoothly forward toward the target and finishes high, with knuckles at shoulder level and racquet head pointing up (thumb up) on the one-handed shot. During the two-handed shot, the hands finish close by the right ear (racquet end cap looks forward to the target).
- Chin should stay close to the front shoulder.
- Wrist should be slightly looser by the end of the stroke in order to relax the arm, but wrist snap is minimal on the one-handed backhand.

Thumb up.

Free hand snaps back, controlling the balance and adding acceleration to the racket (one-handed backhand).

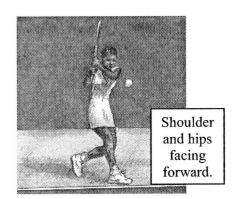

Shoulder and hips facing forward.

7. RECOVERY

- With the forward momentum of the completed follow through, the back foot steps outside towards the sideline, pushing the body to shuffle to the "Recovery Site" or cross stepping to run to the next shot. Open stance players have the advantage of having the outside foot ready to push back to the "Recovery Site," saving one step.[2]

Note: Many players refer to the one-handed backhand as a harder stroke to master, even though swinging away from the body is a more natural motion than the forehand motion. The difference lies in the position of the dominant shoulder (the right shoulder for right-handed players) for each stroke. When the dominant shoulder is in front, like in a one-hand backhand shot, the timing that starts from the racquet back to the completion with the follow through becomes more of an issue (point of contact must be out in front of the body). Likewise, on the forehand stroke, the dominant shoulder is back at the preparation stage, making the shot easier to handle (more time to prepare for the point of contact).

ONE-HAND VS. TWO-HAND

One-Hand Advantages:
(Two-Hand Disadvantages)

- **Better reach**
  The one-handed backhand has far more reach than the two-handed shot. If the two-handed backhand is held with the Continental grip on the bottom hand, the one-handed slice can be utilized, and therefore, there is no reach disadvantage.

- **Ease of footwork**
  A two-handed backhand requires getting closer to the ball than the one-handed shot.

- **Quicker "into the body" return of serve**
  Two-handed players can get jammed more easily.

- **Easy to slice**
  Natural downward swing.

- **Easy to volley**
  Forearm muscles are better prepared for the backhand volley.

- **Ease of high/low shots**
  The one-handed shot has a bigger window for making contact (mid-trunk to mid-thigh) than the restricted two-handed shot (that is why a two-handed player requires quicker and more precise footwork).

Two-Hand Advantages:
(One-Hand Disadvantages)

- **Powerful**
  The use of the second hand makes this stroke an extremely powerful weapon. With the one-handed shot, only the fingertips are behind the grip, requiring a strong forearm to produce a firm shot.

- **Deceiving**
  The two-handed shot is hard to read, and it is easier (than the one-handed shot) to change direction of the ball.

- **Greater Shock Absorption** due to the two hands holding the grip.

- **Sharp Angle Shots**
  Due to the combination of wrist action and firmness, sharper angles can be hit more easily.

BACKHAND VARIATIONS

HIGH BACKHAND

Even though you always should hit the ball at your striking comfort zone (waist level), you will have situations, like a high kicking shot or an approach shot, that will be require you to hit at shoulder level.

Follow the basics for any regular backhand
1. **Split Step / React**
2. **Footwork**
3. **Early Preparation**
4. **Point of Contact**. Not always possible to stop and step, but stress:
    - Hit well out in front and off the front foot especially when attacking forward.
    - Good use of leg extension (getting a lift off the ground from impulse force).
    - Hit *through* with topspin, finishing high and over the ball.
5. **Follow Through**
6. **Recovery**

Note: Most high shots can be hit *off the ground*. Making contact in the air will add more energy (power) to the shot generated from the leg drive (leg muscles) as well as hitting the shot early; all together, a much more offensive shot. Dynamic balance must be maintained throughout the stroke; otherwise, your accuracy will be diminished.

TOPSPIN HIGH BACKHAND *FRONT VIEW*

2. Footwork   **3. Early Preparation**
(1. Split Step / React)

Off the ground.

Maintaining dynamic balance.

4. Point of Contact   **5. Follow Through**   **6. Recovery**

BACKHAND
SLICE

The Great Defense

The slice backhand might not be a powerful shot like the topspin backhand, but it still can be as effective as any other ground stroke when applied at the right time. The slice can keep your opponent off balance by changing pace (floaters as well as aggressive slices) and spin (low bounces). It is just another weapon for your arsenal.

There are other situations where underspin can come in handy. By imparting underspin on an "approach shot," the ball will float deep, buying you time to reach the net, and because of the low bounce, your opponent will be forced to hit up, setting up an easy volley for you. Also, an extreme amount of underspin must be imparted on a drop shot (with a loose wrist) for the ball to bounce low and short and, consequently, to make it unreachable.

Even though the shoulder that holds the racquet is out in front, the slice backhand lets you hit a bit behind the normal topspin shot point of contact (due to the continental grip), thus becoming an excellent defensive shot.[4] Still, footwork and early preparation is essential for this one-handed slice shot.

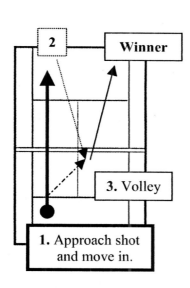

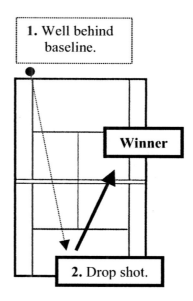

ONE-HANDED SLICE BACKHAND *FRONT VIEW*

3. Early Preparation   4. Stop and Step
(1. Split Step/React   /   2. Footwork)

5. Point of Contact

6. Follow Through

ONE-HANDED SLICE BACKHAND *SIDE VIEW*

4. Stop and Step   5. Point of Contact
(1. Split Step/React / 2. Footwork / 3. Early Preparation)

6. Follow Through

TWO-HANDED SLICE BACKHAND *FRONT VIEW*

4. Stop and Step   **5. Point of contact**
(1. Split Step/React / 2. Footwork / 3. Early Preparation)

6. Follow Through

TWO-HANDED SLICE BACKHAND *SIDE VIEW*

4. Stop and Step   5. Point of Contact
(1. Split Step/React / 2. Footwork / 3. Early Preparation)

6. Follow Through

BACKHAND
SLICE

Square Stance

KEYS:
Balance
Timing

RECOMMENDED GRIPS:
One-handed backhand: Continental[1]
Two-handed backhand: (bottom/top hand) Continental/Eastern forehand, Continental/Semi-Western forehand.[1]

1. **SPLIT STEP / REACT**
   - Get ready.

2. **FOOTWORK**
   - Explosive first step.
   - Get to the ball early.[2]

3. **GOOD EARLY PREPARATION**
   A. Shoulder Turn
   - Hips turn as well.
   - Chin should almost touch the front shoulder to ensure good trunk rotation.

   - Racquet back. Face slightly open and high (above the shoulder).
   - Keep arm and wrist relaxed (Continental grip for one-handed shot).
   - Free hand holds racquet at the throat and helps to take the racquet back (one-handed backhand).

B. Weight
- Weight on back foot (transferred forward as the racquet travels to the point of contact).

C. Knees Bend
- Knees slightly bent.

4. STOP AND STEP OUT IN FRONT

A. Stop and Step
- Stop to hit a controlled, balanced shot and step out in front toward the target.
- For a defensive slice shot, when pulled wide, have a closer stance.[4]

B. Sideways
- Body stays sideways while body motion stops, maintaining good balance.

C. Head Control
- The head should stay steady throughout the shot.

D. Eye Control
- Eyes should be locked on the ball.

E. Forward Motion
- Driving the racquet end cap into the ball (**1**), swing the racquet head down (**2**) and through in a semi-circular motion as your weight transfers *forward* into the ball. Make sure that the racquet head is above the incoming ball before the point of contact in order to generate underspin.
- Hold the racquet with a looser grip to relax the arm and forearm, therefore attaining maximum acceleration.

Hips and shoulders rotate forward.

- Shoulders and hips stay sideways, lining up to the intended target (one-handed backhand).

- Because power is not the main ingredient of the slice backhand, the leg extension (first link of the kinetic body chain) happens only at the end of the stroke as the follow through is performed. Hips and shoulders have very little rotation (one-handed backhand), leaving only gravity (racquet weight), forward momentum (created by the body weight as you hit through), and some leg drive to create power. This forward motion is one smooth, sequenced swing. On the two-handed slice, the hips and shoulders rotate forward, facing the net by completion of the follow through.
- Due to the two hands holding the grip (two-handed backhand), low shots are much more difficult to reach and execute than when using the one-handed slice.

5. POINT OF CONTACT

- Eyes locked on the ball.
- Racquet face slightly open, out in front. The angle of the racquet face depends on the depth and height of the shot needed. For a floater shot the racquet face should be much more open than for an aggressive slice shot (practically perpendicular with the ground at impact).

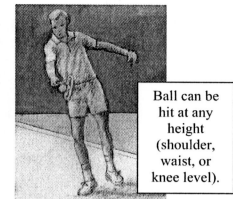

Ball can be hit at any height (shoulder, waist, or knee level).

- Chin should almost touch the front shoulder.
- Arm straight, elbow in (but not locked) and close to trunk.
- Shoulders sideways lining up to the target (one-handed backhand).
- Wrist firm. When underspin is used for a drop shot, or for a slower shot, the wrist should be loose (absorbs energy).
- Weight fully transfers to the front foot. Front knee extends. Back foot is on tiptoe to help maintain good balance.
- Racquet head achieves maximum acceleration at this point. By no means should the racquet slow down.

6. FOLLOW THROUGH

Hips and shoulder facing forward.

- Eyes steady at point of contact (striking zone) for a split second after the ball has left the strings (do not follow the ball with your eyes immediately after point of contact). This will help you control accuracy of the shot, as well as maintain balance.

- Racquet keeps dropping smoothly downward and forward toward the target, brushing the backside of the ball; finish high at shoulder level, with racquet face completely open, controlling depth and height.

- Wrist should be loose to help the racquet create more power and underspin.
- Free hand stays behind, controlling the balance (one-handed backhand).

7. RECOVERY

- Follow the ball if an approach shot is hit or recover to the "Recovery Site" if you stayed on the baseline.[2]

[1] See Chapter 1, **"Grips"**
[2] See Chapter 1, **"Anticipation & Footwork"**
[3] See Chapter 1, **"Backswing Styles"**
[4] See Chapter 1, **"Stances"**
[5] See *Focus on the Ball* in Chapter 6, **"While Playing the Match"**
[6] See *Kinetic Body Chain* in Chapter 1, **"Stances"**

VOLLEY

VOLLEY

The Winning Advantage

To have a winning game, you'll need to be able to come up to the net and finish the point. The volley is a simple mechanical shot. Most of it is just watching the ball (with a quick reaction) and good footwork.

Strategically, coming up to the net will raise your chances of winning a point, because when you hit a quick simple shot (volley) close to the net, you cut off the reaction and execution time of your baseline opponent, who must hit a more complex and time-consuming shot (ground stroke). Also, at the net, you have the possibility of opening up the court with a much more pronounced angle.

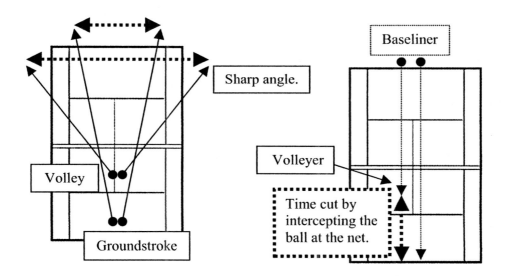

FOREHAND VOLLEY *FRONT VIEW*

1. Split Step / React   **2. Footwork**   **3. Step / 4. Point of Contact**

5. Follow Through   **6. Recovery**

FOREHAND PUNCH VOLLEY *SIDE VIEW*

1. Split Step / React / 2. Footwork / 3. Step

4. Point of Contact   5. Follow Through

6. Recovery

ONE-HANDED BACKHAND PUNCH VOLLEY *FRONT VIEW*

1. Split Step / React   **2. Footwork**

3. Step   **4. Point of Contact**   **5. Follow Through**

ONE-HANDED BACKHAND PUNCH VOLLEY *SIDE VIEW*

1. Split Step / React

2. Footwork　　**3. Step / 4. Point of Contact / 5. Follow Through**

PUNCH VOLLEY

Forehand and One-Handed Backhand

KEYS:
Eye on the ball (early & quick reaction)
Footwork
Timing
Simplicity (no backswing, no follow through)

RECOMMENDED GRIPS:
Continental. Eastern forehand and Eastern backhand for beginners.[1]

1. **SPLIT STEP / REACT**
   - Get ready.[2]
   - Immediate reaction (to forehand or backhand).
   - Racquet and elbows out in front of the body. A common mistake is to split with the elbows tucked to the body, thereby slowing down the volley reaction.

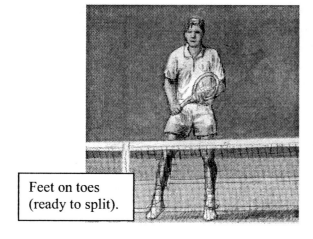

Feet on toes (ready to split).

Ready to react (after the split).

2. **FOOTWORK**
   - First thing, right after the split, is to *set up the racquet*, ready to hit the ball (early and quick reaction), by loading the weight on the outside foot.
   - Cover the shot quickly, moving forward toward the ball, cutting off the angle,[2] with the racquet ready (on the side, facing flat to the ball) to punch (for the backhand volley bend the elbow slightly to facilitate the stroke) and hit aggressively.

Set up the racquet.

Loading the outside foot.

Moving with the racquet ready.

- The free hand helps to control the balance (out in front on the forehand and holds the racquet from the throat on the backhand) as you get to the ball.
- Wrist relaxed.

3. STEP TOWARD THE BALL
- Before contact, step forward toward the ball (medium and low height shots). Step with foot opposite your racquet hand for the forehand volley (left foot) and the same foot as the hand that holds the racquet for the backhand volley (right foot).
- This step will help your shoulder to turn a little sideways, placing your body in a better biomechanical position (mechanically sound shot).
    - **A.** Allows your racquet to go back enough to have a controlled punch (racquet should not go farther back than your back shoulder).
    - **B.** Sets your body in a comfortable position to see the ball well (from the side, not across the strings).
    - **C.** Helps to attack the ball forward (weight transfers forward, creating momentum) and to hit it through without stopping.
- The elbows should be close to the side of the body and slightly out in front to ensure a consistent point of contact.
- On high volleys, you may need to step forward right after contacting the ball, especially when moving forward fast. This way you will be able to control the shot better without pulling down the racquet.

On high volleys, step forward *after* point of contact.

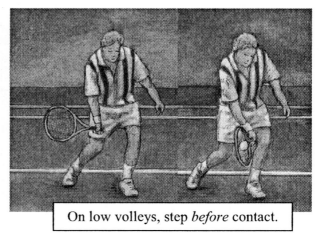

On low volleys, step *before* contact.

- When volleying far from the net (close to the service line) and a *deep shot* is required (first volleys),[2] a slightly longer back swing (further back than your back shoulder) is going to be necessary; just be aware that the longer the backswing, the harder to control the point of contact (too much power).

4. POINT OF CONTACT
- Eyes locked on the ball.
- Without completely stopping, punch through the ball.
- The shoulder should be slightly sideways and the point of contact should be aligned with the front shoulder (or just in front) for a more aggressive volley.
- Racquet arm should be straight but not locked (at the elbow).
- Racquet head should be higher than the wrist, forming a "V" between the racquet and the forearm. This "V" will provide stability, control, and power. That is why it is important to maintain this "V" in all situations, especially on low shots.
- On low volleys, keeping the "V" up will keep the racquet face straight, and help the ball to clear the net low. When you are at the net, the last thing you want is to volley up, leaving your opponent with an easy put-away shot. Try to keep the "V" by getting low with a wide step forward, and bending down from your knees (back knee will be almost touching the ground).
- On high volleys, drive the racquet end cap into the ball first, and then the racquet head should impact the ball.

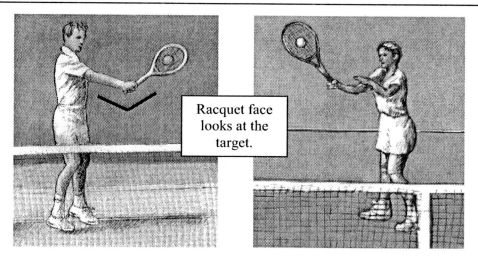

Racquet face looks at the target.

Keeping Up the "V"

Note: When punching the ball, make sure not to swing the racquet. The punch happens by stepping forward towards the ball and keeping the arm firm (firm wrist), making a consistent point of contact.

- A small amount of underspin or slice should be imparted to the ball. The spin will help control the flight of the ball, and it will also add a low bounce, forcing your opponent to hit the ball up, which will give you an easy put-away second volley. Be careful not to scoop the ball to impart spin. Instead, think of punching the ball through with the racquet face straight (on edge), and then slightly open the racquet face as the ball leaves your strings (not a downward swing).

Wrist firm.

Elbow in and forward

Free hand out in front.

Wrist laid back (hyperextended), on the *forehand* stroke due to the Continental grip.

Note: Make sure not to slap at the ball (wrist action). This will create an inconsistent, weak, angular shot.

- Free hand stays out in front for the forehand and back for the backhand, controlling the body motion and balance.
- Unless you need to absorb energy for a touch shot like a drop shot or drop volley (loose wrist), keep your wrist firm for a crisp shot.

Remember: Don't look for *power* on volleys but for *control* (placement). Power will be generated using the energy (speed) of the incoming ball and your forward momentum (moving and stepping forward with a firm wrist).

5. FOLLOW THROUGH

- Eyes stay steady at point of contact (striking zone) for a split second after the ball has left the strings (do not follow the ball with your eyes immediately after point of contact). This will help you control the accuracy of your shot, as well as maintain balance.
- Wrist relaxed.
- Follow the ball with the strings just slightly forward and through the ball for a compact feel (bottom edge of racquet follows forward slightly, opening the racquet face). Make sure to do this slight angle change of the racquet face *immediately after* the point of contact (imparting underspin) and *not before* (that would create a floater volley which is too easy to return).

Bottom racquet edge follows the ball.

Right elbow (racquet arm) in and forward (forehand volley).

- Keep your head still throughout the stroke to maintain dynamic balance.

6. RECOVERY

- Racquet quickly recovers to the center of the body and above the net on low volleys to prepare for the next shot.
- The back foot steps outside toward the sideline, pushing the body to shuffle to the "Recovery Site."[2]

Racquet recovers to the center of the body.

Back foot steps outside towards the sideline.

VOLLEY VARIATIONS

"RIGHT AT YOUR BODY" VOLLEY

Most often this shot must to be played as a one-hand block backhand volley. Using the racquet as a shield, you can defend your body and win the point with this quick reaction shot.

The forehand block volley will only be used when the ball is coming straight at your right armpit (right-handed players). If the ball comes right at your body but not at a high speed (no pace), step away from the ball and treat it as a regular forehand volley, trying to step forward if possible. When the ball comes right at you with a lot of pace, it becomes a very difficult shot to control and the only way to effectively volley it is by dodging the ball with the shoulders (right shoulder pivots backward, trying to avoid the ball). At the same time the racquet takes its place (where right shoulder was), making a solid blocking volley (point of contact will be slightly behind but aligned with your head).

Remember: However you choose to take this "right at your body" volley (as a forehand or as a backhand), make sure there is no hesitation, only a quick reaction.

BLOCK VOLLEY

Quick Switch from forehand to backhand and vice versa.

KEYS:
Split Step Reaction
Simplicity (just a block)

RECOMMENDED GRIP:
Continental[1]

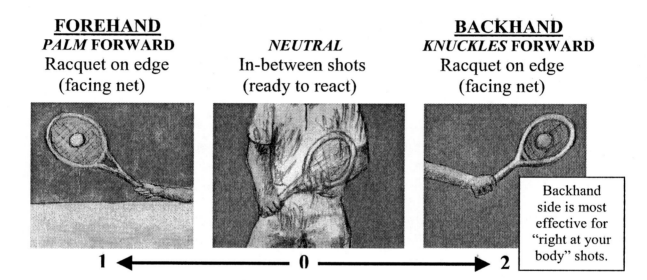

FOREHAND	*NEUTRAL*	**BACKHAND**
PALM FORWARD	In-between shots	*KNUCKLES* FORWARD
Racquet on edge	(ready to react)	Racquet on edge
(facing net)		(facing net)

1 ⟵————— 0 —————⟶ 2

Backhand side is most effective for "right at your body" shots.

A. SPLIT STEP / REACT
   Racquet in the center of your body, ready to react, at neutral position (**0**).

B. QUICK READY
   Work with your palm forward (**1**) for the forehand or knuckles forward (**2**) for the backhand to develop a quick reaction as you load the outside foot.

TWO-HANDED BACKHAND VOLLEY

Though there is nothing wrong volleying with two hands, especially if you've just started to play the game, the one-handed volley has many more advantages than the two-handed shot.

Two-hands on the grip will shorten your reach, jam you on shots "right at your body," slow you down on quick exchanges, and will make your "serve and volley" game completely unsuccessful (extremely difficult on low volleys). On the other hand, it is a comfortable, powerful shot (waist and high shots). However, power is not an issue on volleys.

Remember, if you have a two-handed backhand ground stroke, the two-handed backhand volley will come naturally. Developing the one-handed shot will not be easy (dominant hand forearm muscles might need conditioning). Start by preparing the shot with two hands **(1, 2)**, and then as you make contact with the ball **(3)** release the top hand **(4)**. Once the forearm muscles get stronger, you will be able to control the stroke better.

Note: The recommended grips for the two-handed backhand volley with the top hand release **(4)** are any combination that holds the bottom hand with "Continental" grip.[1] This grip will allow you to control the shot by imparting some slice without compromising power. If the top hand is not released, play with the same grip used for the two-handed backhand stroke.

LOB VOLLEY

The lob volley is a combination of the lob and the volley used as a variation of the regular punch or drop volley. Even though it is considered a volley because the ball is hit in the air without the bounce, this shot is more of a control-touch shot than an offensive put-away volley. The ball is contacted with an open-faced racquet and a firm wrist in order to pinpoint the lob.

It is mostly used when your opponent is running forward to get a drop shot or low volley and is especially effective on clay, when changing direction is most difficult.

DROP VOLLEY

The drop volley is a shot that, when played at the right time, has the power to confuse your opponent, disrupt his rhythm, and finish the point easily (usually your opponent expects a forceful offensive volley, not a ball that just clears the net). However, make sure your opponent is behind the baseline (some players are extremely fast), and keep up the element of surprise (don't overuse it).

Also, notice that the most effective surface for a drop volley is on slow courts, like clay or Har-Tru, because the ball, which carries heavy underspin and no power, will bounce very low on the slow surface, making a tough shot to reach, practically unreachable.

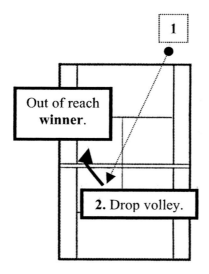

FOREHAND DROP VOLLEY *FRONT VIEW*

1. Split Step / React   2. Footwork

3. Step / 4. Point of Contact   5. Absorb Shock

FOREHAND DROP VOLLEY *SIDE VIEW*

1. Split Step / React

2. Footwork / 3. Step   **4. Point of Contact**   **5. Absorb Shock**

ONE-HANDED BACKHAND DROP VOLLEY *FRONT VIEW*

1. Split Step/React   **2. Footwork**

3. Step / 4. Point of Contact 5. Absorb Shock

ONE-HANDED BACKHAND DROP VOLLEY *SIDE VIEW*

3. Step   **4. Contact**   **5. Absorb Shock**
(1. Split Step/React / 2. Footwork)

DROP VOLLEY

Forehand and One-Handed Backhand

KEYS:
Timing
Loose Wrist

RECOMMENDED GRIP:
Continental[1]

- Same procedure as a punch volley, but before making contact with the ball, loosen up the grip to have a relaxed wrist and absorb most of the energy of the ball.

Loose wrist.

- There is no follow through with this shot. The racquet dies right after the point of contact, insuring no transfer of energy into the ball.

STAB VOLLEY

Forehand and One-Handed Backhand

A stab volley is an emergency shot that, in most cases, will result in a drop volley. The difference is that a stab volley is a reaction shot; it is not premeditated. Footwork is not effective because the ball is too far away; therefore, a lunge is necessary.[2] The racquet should be kept straight (on edge) throughout the point of contact, and the wrist loosens up right after, producing a stabbing motion (underspin), and a drop volley.

Move first with the outside foot as you push off with the other foot.

1. Lunge   **2. Point of Contact (Stab)**

Free hand controls the body balance.

3. Absorb Shock

[1] See Chapter 1, **"Grips"**
[2] See Chapter 1, **"Anticipation & Footwork"**
[3] See Chapter 5, **"Volley Strategy"**

<u>SERVE</u>

SERVE

The Killer Strength

The serve can be the greatest weapon, but it also is a double-edged sword. If your service is effective (powerful, good placement, spin variety), it can open up the point aggressively and, therefore, make it easy to control and win the point. On the other hand, if your serve is poorly executed, your opponent will take charge of the point, no matter how aggressive your strokes are.

Psychologically, the serve can be a great confidence builder, or buster. When your serve is on, your game and strategy will fall into place, but when your serve is off, you can lose all of your confidence in your strokes and game plan.

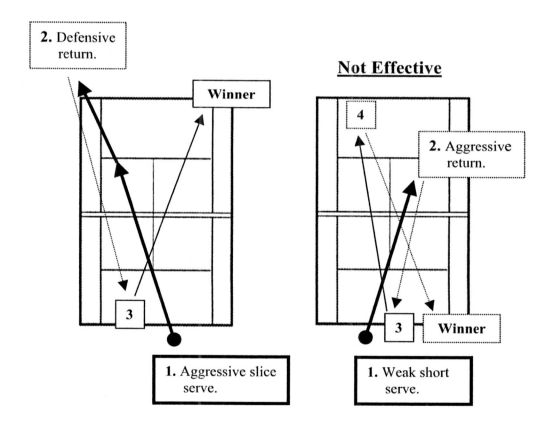

FIRST SERVE *FRONT VIEW*

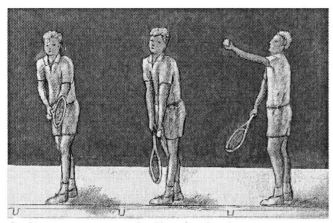

1. Stance   **2. Begin Swing**

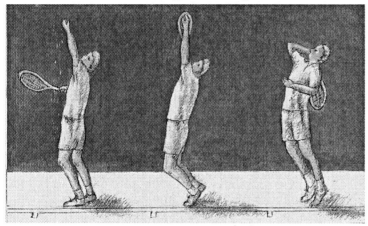

3. Upward Motion

4. Point of Contact   **5. Follow Through**

FIRST SERVE *SIDE VIEW*

1. Stance   **2. Begin Swing**

3. Upward Motion

4. Point of Contact   **5. Follow Through**

FIRST SERVE

KEYS:
Rhythm & Timing
Loose & Relaxed (Smooth Swing)
Balance
Controlled Toss
Simplicity

RECOMMENDED GRIPS:
Continental. Eastern backhand, Eastern forehand (beginners).[1]

1. STANCE
- Stand comfortably (loose & relaxed), about one foot from the center mark, with fairly straight posture.
- Knees slightly bent.
- Feet shoulder width apart. Front foot is about an inch behind the baseline at a 45-degree angle to it. The back foot is parallel to the baseline. Toes (both feet) should be lined up towards the intended target.
- Face sideways. Sideways shoulder and hips ensure a good body rotation, which will generate angular momentum.
- Hands together, racquet pointing to the aimed service box.
- Weight starts on the front foot.
- Wrist relaxed.

2. BEGIN SWING

- Start routine (always the same way).
- Hands start together.
- Racquet is out in front and the weight is on the front foot.
- Hands drop down together and start a *slow, smooth,* upward motion with the racquet arm slightly delayed (**B**). Some players manage to lift both arms up at the same time, which is all right as long as you can keep good smooth rhythm (but it slows down racquet head acceleration).
- The weight shifts from the front foot (**A**) quickly to the back foot (**B**) and then back to the front foot (**C**) in a rocking motion.

Keep the knuckles up on the backswing.

90°

A   B   C

- Holding the ball by the fingertips, very gently and slowly lift the hand slightly forward, aiming to the right net post (45-degree angle with the baseline).[2] The ball should be tossed with the arm straight (lift from the shoulder), in a straight upward motion, without bending the elbow or wrist, avoiding any kind of spin on the ball. Release the ball above eye level (**B**) to ensure a straight up toss. This arm stays up for a split second after the release, then comes down to the chest (at point of contact). The ball should be placed as high as the height of the tip of the racquet stretched up, this way the ball drops a couple of inches to the center of the racquet (point of contact) without picking up any speed from the vertical fall (gravity).
- How to take the racquet back (backswing serve) is a matter of style. Some have it long and some have it compact, but all backswings should be smooth, rhythmically correct, and should get to the same position (**C**).
- Left hip (front hip) shifts forward (**C**).
- Elbow up (90 degrees between the elbow and trunk).

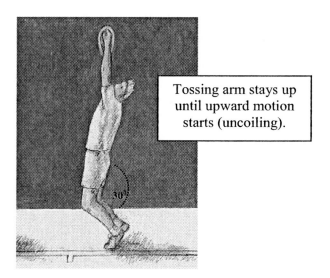

Tossing arm stays up until upward motion starts (uncoiling).

- At this point, the knees bend down, about 30 degrees, and shoulders should be fully rotated, about 140 degrees with the baseline (coil), for maximum power (acceleration) production.

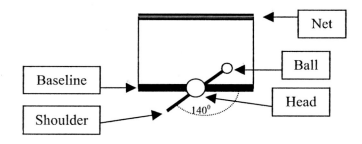

Net

Ball

Baseline

Shoulder

Head

140°

COILING
(*Top View*)
- Weight and hip shift forward.
- Shoulder rotation.
- Elbow up.
- Tossing arm up.

- As the ball gets to the point of contact area, the racquet drops behind the back. The elbow stays up 90 degrees or more from the trunk, pointing back.

3. UPWARD MOTION

- First, the knees straighten up, pushing off the front foot and starting the kinetic chain of energy production. This exploding, upward force will impel the body off the ground.
- Then, as the hips and shoulders rotate forward, the body weight is added to the ground forces (body moves forward to the tossed ball) generated by the kinetic chain.
- Elbow points up and moves forward with the shoulder rotation. The racquet is still behind the back but away from it (no back scratch), getting ready for maximum acceleration. Note that the palm of the hand that holds the racquet always stays facing down (knuckles up), canceling any extra forward wrist movement, and increasing the spin and *pronation* (note that the racquet *edge* is facing up).

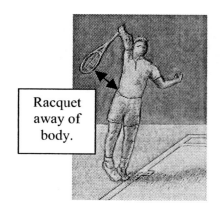

Racquet away of body.

Racquet *edge* faces up (not the strings).

- Arm and wrist extend up as racquet accelerates and applies *spin* to the ball at point of contact.[3]

4. POINT OF CONTACT

- Shoulder and hip are completely rotated, facing the net.
- Palm and racquet turn inward for full pronation.

Racquet *edge* turns inward, making the strings face the target and stroking the ball.

- Make contact when the ball reaches the peak of the toss or just starts to come down (the ball carries no speed at the peak or very little as it starts to come down).
- Hit up and forward (all the energy is concentrated to the point of contact, not to the service box).
- Racquet, arm, trunk, and front foot are almost in straight line.
- Thumb of hand that holds the racquet points up.
- Wrist firm.
- Racquet face looks at target for perfect aiming. At this point racquet head reaches maximum acceleration.

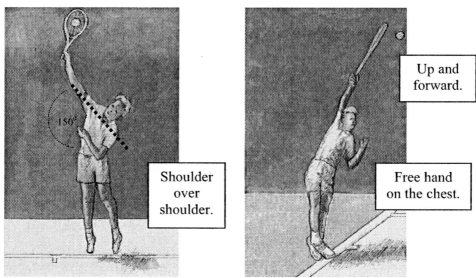

150°

Shoulder over shoulder.

Up and forward.

Free hand on the chest.

- Shoulder is almost in a vertical position (150 degrees or more between the arm and trunk), and the right shoulder reaching as high as possible (the higher the reach, the greater the margin for net clearance).

- Tossing arm moves into the chest, so racquet arm snaps (accelerates).

5. FOLLOW THROUGH

- Right after contact, the racquet continues forward as *chin stays up* (this prevents the ball from dropping into the net).

Inner racquet edge turns inward (pronates) as the strings follow the ball.

- Wrist snaps (looser wrist), adding speed to the ball (last link of kinetic chain). Thumb points down and elbow up.

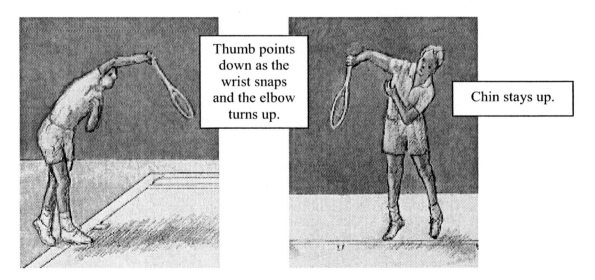

Thumb points down as the wrist snaps and the elbow turns up.

Chin stays up.

- First, land on front foot inside the court, then the back foot comes along. Let forward momentum carry you forward.[4]

- Right shoulder completely rotates forward.
- Racquet finishes on the left side of the body (flush with the leg).

6. RECOVERY
- Continue moving forward for serve and volley game.[5]
- Make several splits steps, backing up quickly for baseline game.

FOR MORE POWER

- Make sure your weight is fully transferred forward (fall inside the court after point of contact).
- Focus on acceleration, not on strength, don't muscle the shot.
- Make sure motion is smooth and continuous. Do not stop when racquet is behind the back.
- Rotate shoulders well (150-degree angle with the baseline) and keep racquet away from the back when coiling (shoulder rotation).
- Use kinetic body chain as the source of power (ground forces + body links = acceleration).
- Focus on acceleration towards the point of contact, not the service box.
- As with any other stroke, you can manipulate equipment to adapt to your game style. To gain more power, lower the string tension (trampoline effect) and/or add lead tape to the head of the racquet, around the 9 and 3 o'clock spots. Also, you may consider switching to a stiffer (but heavier) racquet, maybe even a longer-bodied racquet (longer than the traditional 27" long) with an oversize head.

SERVE VARIATIONS

SPINS AND SECOND SERVES

Good servers not only have the ability to place the serve effectively, they can also keep their opponent guessing by changing pace and spin. Mixing up the service is a must for an advanced player.

Many players believe that a second serve is like a first one but slower. If you follow that thought, your serve will look more like a weak push than an aggressive delivery. Most of the ingredients of the first serve make up the second serve. However, some adjustments (grips, ball toss placement, focus of acceleration-spins, etc.) are needed (as discussed in Chapter 1, "Spins").

Focus of Acceleration-Spins
The major difference between a topspin first serve and a topspin second serve is the focus of acceleration. The direction of the energy is the same, but for a first serve, the forward vector (hollow arrow) is the focus of acceleration. In other words, the racquet should accelerate faster at that point and in that direction. For a second serve, the focus of acceleration is the brushing behind the ball vector (black arrow), and therefore, more spin than power will be created, producing a higher percentage second serve.

> ***Energy Vectors***
> Racquet face should follow the direction of the vector (gray arrow), extending upward with the body and arm, and brushing the backside of the ball *7 to 1* (black arrow) with the wrist. After contact, the wrist snaps and racquet follows straight forward (hollow arrow) to the target.

Remember: Do not slow down your 2nd serve; instead replace *power by spin*.

---

[1] See Chapter 1, **"Grips"**
[2] See *Placement of the Toss* in Chapter 1, **"Spins"**
[3] See *Applying Spin on the Serve* in Chapter 1, **"Spins"**
[4] See *Serve Footwork Patterns* in Chapter 1, **"Anticipation & Footwork"**
[5] See Chapter 3, **"Serve and Volley"**

<u>RETURN OF SERVE</u>

RETURN OF SERVE

The Silent Weapon

The return of serve should be treated as more than just another shot. A good "returner" can steal the momentum from a server and make him pay for a weak second serve. Generally speaking, it is important for any player to develop a good return, but it's essential for a player who doesn't own a big serve: by breaking the server, the returner can be more relaxed when it's time for him to serve. Two of the best all time returners, Andre Agassi and Jimmy Connors, both relied on the return of serve to keep the pressure on the server and finally break his game (note that they were not known for killer serves).

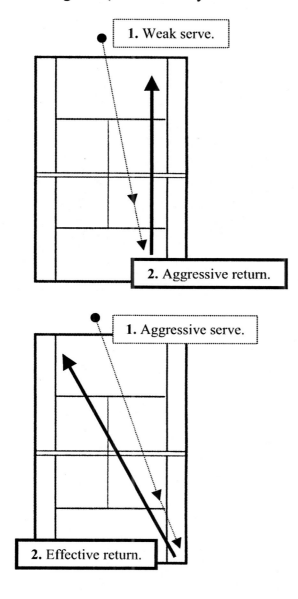

FOREHAND RETURN *FRONT VIEW*

1. Ready Position / Split Step / React   **2. Shoulder Turn**

3. Step   **4. Point of Contact**

5. Follow Through   **6. Recovery**

FOREHAND RETURN *SIDE VIEW*

1. Ready Position / Split Step / React

2. Shoulder Turn   **3. Step**   **4. Point of Contact**

5. Follow Through   **6. Recovery**

ONE-HANDED BACKHAND RETURN *FRONT VIEW*

1. Ready / Split Step / React   **2. Shoulder Turn**

3. Step   **4. Point of Contact**

5. Follow Through   **6. Recovery**

ONE-HANDED BACKHAND RETURN *SIDE VIEW*

1. Ready Position / Split Step / React **2. Shoulder Turn**

3. Step **4. Point of Contact**

5. Follow Through **6. Recovery**

TWO-HANDED BACKHAND RETURN *FRONT VIEW*

1. Ready Position / Split Step / React

2. Shoulder Turn / 3. Step / 4. Point of Contact

5. Follow Through   6. Recovery

TWO-HANDED BACKHAND RETURN *SIDE VIEW*

1. Ready Position / Split Step / React   2. Shoulder Turn

3. Step   4. Point of Contact   5. Follow Through

6. Recovery

RETURN OF SERVE
FLAT OR TOPSPIN

Forehand and Backhand

KEYS:
Quick Early Reaction
Aggressiveness
Firm Blocking Wrist (Compact Backswing)

RECOMMENDED GRIPS:
Same grips used for topspin forehand and backhand groundstrokes.[1]

1. READY POSITION[2] / SPLIT STEP / REACT

- Stand in a spot where you can cover the forehand as well as the backhand return, usually a foot or two away from the intersection of the baseline and the singles sideline. Waiting position can vary depending on the depth, speed, and spin of the opponent's serve, but for the first serve, it is commonly about one to two feet behind the baseline, and for the second serve, a foot inside the baseline. As rule of thumb, if you need more time to react, back up as much as necessary in order to place the ball back in play. If the serve is slow, move up as much as you can in order to hit the ball on the rise and attack.[3]
- Racquet out in front, preferably in the center of your body (neutral position).
- Wrist relaxed.
- Free hand (fingertips) holds the racquet at its throat.
- Knees bend for low center of balance, and upper body leans slightly forward from the waist (for quick reaction).
- Eyes fix on opponent's toss and point of contact.

- **Footwork:**
  A. Traditional

- Feet comfortably apart, about shoulder width and parallel to the baseline.
- Split step forward with both feet just before opponent hits the ball.[4]
- Quickly react for a forehand or a backhand.

B. One Foot Out

- One foot is out in front. It doesn't matter which one is out as long as it's always the same one (get into a routine).
- Step forward with the back foot before the opponent hits the ball and split step forward.[4]
- Quickly react for a forehand or a backhand.

2. SHOULDER TURN

- Load the outside foot by rotating the shoulders and hips accordingly.

Free hand out in front.

Free hand helps on the backswing.

- Racquet goes back with a *compact backswing* for a quicker reaction.[5] Focus is on quick shoulder turn rather than racquet back. Shoulder turn will guarantee enough power without compromising control. How far the racquet should go back depends on the serve. As a rule of thumb, the faster the serve, the more compact the backswing should be. For some very fast serves, use a block type return.

3. STEP

- Step forward to get some momentum behind the ball and generate pace.
- On very fast serves when a quick reaction is the only way to return, hit the ball in open stance.[2]

4. POINT OF CONTACT

- Eyes locked on the ball.
- Knees extend, hips and shoulder rotate forward (forehand and two-handed backhand), and with a firm, tight grip, block the ball. On the one-handed backhand, hips and shoulders stay sideways, lining up with the target area.
- Racquet face aims at the target area.
- Free hand snaps backward as racquet makes contact with the ball, helping to maintain control and balance (one-handed backhand).

5. FOLLOW THROUGH

- Racquet face follows forward toward the target.
- Racquet finishes over the shoulder, imparting some topspin. On faster serves, it is better to use a block return, finishing with the racquet firm out in front (like a volley).
- Dynamic balance throughout the stroke must be maintained. Keeping the swing compact and simple will allow you to gain accuracy and consistency, regardless of the speed of the serve, and it will also help you recover quickly for the next shot.

- Free hand remains back throughout the follow through (one-handed backhand).

Head steady throughout the follow through.

6. RECOVERY

- Immediately with the forward momentum of the follow through, the back foot steps outside, pushing back to the "Recovery Site" or follow your return forward attacking the net.[4]

RETURN VARIATIONS

CHIP RETURN

The chip return is a great weapon for returning fast, powerful serves and for use against "Serve & Volley" players. Mostly used on the backhand side (one-handed slice[6]), this shot will keep the ball low (slicing effect) forcing a "Serve & Volley" player to volley up, and it will prevent a baseliner from attacking as easily as he would, with a high bouncing return. Most importantly, this return gives you more time to charge the net, because the floating effect of the underspin takes longer to reach the opponent's side. Therefore, you can reach a more aggressive position closer to the net.

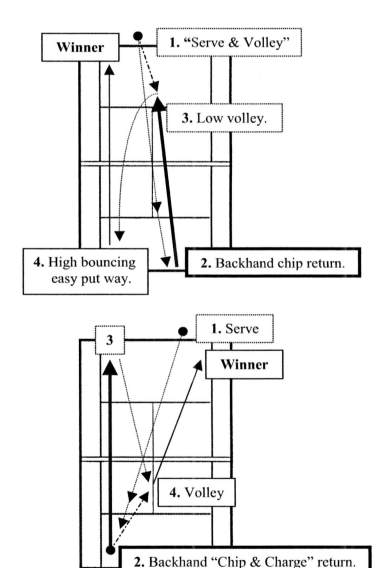

CHIP RETURN OF SERVE *SIDE VIEW*

1. Ready Position   **Split Step**

React   **2. Shoulder Turn**

3. Step / 4. Contact   5. Follow Through

CHIP RETURN OF SERVE

One-Handed Backhand and Forehand

KEYS:
Quick and Early Reaction
High Preparation
Firm Blocking Wrist
Balance

RECOMMENDED GRIP:
Continental[1]

1. **READY POSITION[2] / SPLIT STEP / REACT**
   - Quickly react to the opponent's serve as the ball leaves the strings, loading the outside foot.

2. **SHOULDER TURN**
   - Same as a regular return, but racquet is prepared above shoulder level.

3. **STEP**
   - Step forward to get some momentum behind the ball and generate pace and spin.

4. **POINT OF CONTACT**
   - Eyes locked on the ball.
   - Meet the ball well out in front.
   - Knees extend as the ball is punched like a volley.
   - Arm straight.
   - Wrist firm.
   - Impart a bit of slice by slightly opening the racquet face.

- Shoulders are sideways.
- Free hand stays back, maintaining balance.

5. FOLLOW THROUGH
- Racquet face and arm continues forward toward target.
- Racquet face opens as ball leaves the racquet, right after the point of contact.
- Weight completely transfers to front foot.

Head steady
throughout the
follow through.

6. RECOVERY
- Recover to the "Recovery Site"[4] or charge the net.

---

[1] See Chapter 1, **"Grips"**
[2] See Chapter 1, **"Stances"**
[3] See Chapter 5, **"Return of Serve Strategy"**
[4] See Chapter 1, **"Anticipation & Footwork"**
[5] See Chapter 1, **"Backswing Styles"**
[6] See Chapter 2, **"Slice Backhand"**

<u>OVERHEAD</u>

OVERHEAD SMASH

The Shot of No Return

Today, winning tennis just from the baseline is almost impossible, but attacking the net is risky if you do not own an effective and powerful overhead.

The motion of the overhead is similar to the serve. However, there are a number of differences that a player must know in order to own a consistent overhead. One important point is that the overhead ball is derived from an opponent's *lob*, consequently, the smasher must get into a position to hit it (on the serve, the ball is in control, in server's hand). Also, consider that the higher that ball is, the more downward acceleration (gravity) will affect the ball. Therefore, good timing is critical, which is why the backswing of an overhead should be abbreviated.

The overhead, like the serve, is a confidence booster. When consistent, well placed, and with a good amount of power, it can definitely be called "the shot of no return."

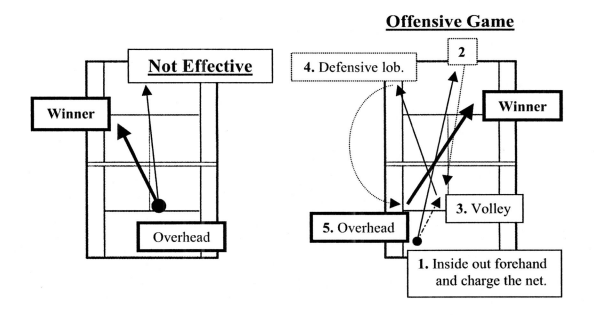

OVERHEAD SMASH *SIDE VIEW*

2. Recognizing a Lob   3. Footwork
(1. Split Step / React)

4. Upward Motion   5. Point of Contact

6. Follow Through

OVERHEAD

KEYS:
Early Preparation
Quick Footwork
Good Timing

RECOMMENDED GRIP:
Continental, Eastern forehand (beginners).[1]

1. SPLIT STEP / REACT
- Get ready.[2]

2. RECOGNIZING A LOB
- Quickly recognize and react to opponent's lob.

- Step back with the right foot (this action allows the shoulders and hips to get sideways, getting ready for easy and quick movement[2] in order to get under the ball). As you step back, the racquet goes back in an abbreviated backswing and the free hand extends up. Fingertips point to the ball, as if trying to catch the ball. This will help you get under the ball more quickly and precisely.

3. FOOTWORK

- Good footwork is essential for an effective overhead. Proper footwork is needed to get the body into position. As the ball reaches its height, quickly move back and get under it as if it was going to fall on top of your head or chest, or place yourself under the ball as if it was a ball toss on a serve.[2]

4. COILING

- Racquet goes behind and away from the back.
- Elbow is high, pointing up.
- Shoulders and hips are sideways.
- Knees bend (not low).
- Weight is off the back foot.

Keep the back fairly straight to hit a flat overhead.

5. UPWARD MOTION

- Knees extend. If you need to jump, keep dynamic balance.[2]
- Free hand is out in front.

6. POINT OF CONTACT

- Eyes locked on the ball.
- Shoulder and hips rotate forward, facing the net.
- Weight shifts forward. If a jump is necessary, keep dynamic balance.
- Racquet, arm, and body fully extend (right shoulder stretches upward).
- Point of contact happens in front and slightly to the right.
- Palm and racquet pronate.[3]
- Free hand goes to the chest (this stops the shoulder, producing a whipping effect).
- For aiming, use the palm holding the racquet. Wherever the palm faces, the racquet face will direct the ball.
- If close to the net (around the service line), clearance of the net is not an issue, so hit the overhead *flat*.
- Chin up.

Back straight.

7. FOLLOW THROUGH

- Wrist snaps, adding speed to the ball (last link of kinetic chain).
- Racquet continues forward as pronation continues.
- Chin stays up.
- Wrist relaxes and arm follows to the left side of the body (flush with the leg).
- Back foot steps forward.

Thumb down and elbow up.

Front View   *Side View*

8. RECOVERY

- Split step and get ready for a surprise return.

OVERHEAD VARIATION

BACKHAND SMASH

- Difficult shot (requires strong shoulder and back muscles).
- Use only when a regular overhead is not an option (opponent's lob is well into your backhand side).
- Use continental or eastern backhand grip.

1. After the split step, react and move under the ball.
2. Turn sideways into a backhand position (racquet is back, elbow is up and pointing to the ball).
3. With the weight transferred onto the back foot, push off and snap into the high ball.
4. Contact the ball as high as possible and slightly in front of the body. The free hand snaps back, producing a whipping effect.
5. Right after the point of contact, the arm and racquet follow the ball (as much as possible), finishing with the back practically facing the net.

[1] See Chapter 1, **"Grips"**
[2] See Chapter 1, **"Anticipation & Footwork"**
[3] See *Palm Pronation* in Chapter 2, **"Serve"**

CHAPTER 3

<u>*TRANSITIONAL GAME*</u>
HOW TO GET TO THE NET

APPROACH SHOT

APPROACH SHOT

The Aggressor

Many times, the difference between winning and losing lies in taking or not taking an opportunity. When the opponent hits a short ball or weak shot, you should attack by moving in, hitting a deep approach shot and finishing the point at the net. Therefore, the key for success at the net lies in the ability to perform the approach shot offensively (deep), with no hesitation, and strategically well placed.

Attacking the short ball and moving fast to the net should be an instinct, not premeditated. This action puts so much pressure on your opponent that you will force him into an error or set yourself up for an easy volley.

The approach shot can be hit in many ways. The one-handed slice is usually used on the backhand side because it helps you gain time while moving to the net. Since it is a low bouncing shot[1], it will force your opponent to hit up, setting you up for an easy volley. On the forehand side a slice can also be used, but an aggressive topspin approach shot will put your opponent into a more vulnerable position (biomechanically speaking, the forehand slice is not as smooth as the backhand slice due to the position of the shoulder when the shot is executed).

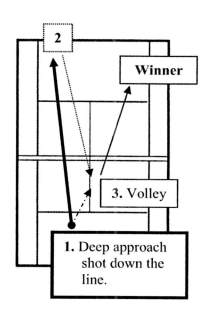

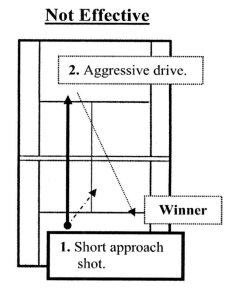

Not Effective

FOREHAND TOPSPIN APPROACH SHOT *SIDE VIEW*

2. Early Recognition / 3. Footwork / 4. Backswing
(1. Split Step / React)

5. Point of Contact   **6. Follow Through**

7. Keep Moving   **8. Split Step**

FOREHAND SLICE APPROACH SHOT *FRONT VIEW*

1. Split Step / React   2. Early Recognition   3. Footwork / 4. Backswing

5. Point of Contact   6. Follow Through

7. Keep Moving   **8. Split Step**

FOREHAND SLICE APPROACH SHOT *SIDE VIEW*

2. Early Recognition / 3. Footwork   4. Compact Backswing
(1. Split Step / React)

5. Point of Contact   6. Follow Through

7. Keep Moving

BACKHAND SLICE APPROACH SHOT *FRONT VIEW*

3. Footwork / 4. Compact Backswing
(1. Split Step / React / 2. Early Recognition)

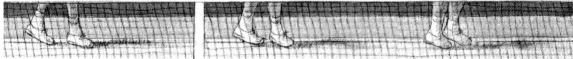

5. Point of Contact   **6. Follow Through**

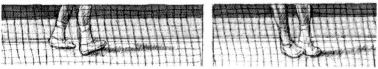

7. Keep Moving

197

BACKHAND SLICE APPROACH SHOT *SIDE VIEW*

1. Split Step / React   2. Early Recognition / 3. Footwork

4. Compact Backswing   5. Point of Contact

6. Follow Through   7. Keep Moving

TWO-HAND BACKHAND SLICE APPROACH SHOT *SIDE VIEW*

2. Early Recognition / 3. Footwork   4. Compact Backswing
(1. Split Step / React)

5. Point of Contact   6. Follow Through

7. Keep Moving   8. Split Step

APPROACH SHOT
TOPSPIN and SLICE

Forehand and Backhand

KEYS:
Early Recognition
Hit through the shot (without stopping)
Placement

RECOMMENDED GRIPS:
Forehand and one-handed backhand: Continental for slice. Eastern, Semi-Western forehand/backhand, and Western forehand for topspin.[2]
Two-handed backhand: (bottom/top hand) Continental/Eastern forehand, Continental/Semi-Western forehand.[2]

1. SPLIT STEP / REACT
* Get ready.[3]

2. EARLY RECOGNITION
* Right off the split step, recognize the short ball early.[4]

3. FOOTWORK
* Move into the ball quickly so contact is made at the peak of the bounce (maximum height).

- On the forehand slice, the back foot steps in front of the front foot to hit through the ball, maintaining dynamic balance (no stopping).[3]

4. COMPACT BACKSWING

- A shorter backswing (straight back[1]) will help you get ready earlier, and because control (placement) is more important than power, this compact backswing will produce a more consistent shot.
- Racquet head should be at shoulder level in order to slice the ball. Use a regular backswing for a drive topspin approach shot.
- Eyes locked on the ball.
- Knees slightly bent.

High backswing for slice.

Compact backswing.

5. POINT OF CONTACT

- Eyes locked on the ball.
- Weight is well on the front foot and point of contact is well out in front. On the slice forehand, hitting the ball off the back foot will allow you to stroke through the ball (due to the position of the dominant shoulder), while maintaining dynamic balance.
- Make contact at the peak of the bounce (maximum height), so your opponent has less time to get to a better position.
- Brush the backside and under the ball, to impart underspin, or brush over the ball for topspin.[5]
- Hit through the shot, without completely stopping. Just slow down, maintaining dynamic balance.
- Keep head still throughout the shot.
- Wrist firm.

- On the one-handed backhand approach shot, the free hand remains behind, helping to maintain dynamic balance.

6. FOLLOW THROUGH

- Compact but full. If it is too long it might slow down progressing to the net.
- Knees extend to add some power to the shot, but mostly to keep momentum moving forward.

7. KEEP MOVING

- Keep moving forward toward the target, following the flight of the ball and, therefore, covering any possible angles of return.

Keep moving and quickly accelerate, following the ball.

Head still.

Carrioca step.

- The one-handed backhand requires more efficient footwork (carrioca[3]), which enables you to keep the shoulders sideways as the shot is performed and, consequently, remain well balanced throughout the shot.

8. SPLIT STEP

- Get ready for the volley.[3]

[1] See Chapter 1, **"Backswing Styles"**
[2] See Chapter 1, **"Grips"**
[3] See Chapter 1, **"Anticipation & Footwork"**
[4] See Chapter 5, **"Approach Shot Strategy"**
[5] See Chapter 1, **"Spins"**

SWINGING VOLLEY

SWINGING VOLLEY

The Swinging Advantage

The swinging volley, played mostly from mid-court, is not a shot for everybody. This shot requires precise timing, good eyes and excellent footwork. Nevertheless, if you practice and master this stroke, you will have another way to get to the net but more aggressively than with the approach shot because you can make contact much closer to the net (no bounce), reducing the opponent's time to react.

Though the swinging volley can be hit from both sides (forehand and backhand), the backhand is hard to perform with consistency. This shot is real tricky to master because it can be hit at any height (it is hard to judge the point of contact), which makes it very difficult for both the two-handed backhand (especially the high shots) and the one-handed backhand (weak). The comfort striking zone for a swinging volley is around waist level (like a groundstroke but without a ball bounce). Nevertheless, the higher the point of contact, the better (with a higher point of contact the net clearance becomes less of an issue).

Modern tennis has become a much more aggressive game than what it used to be. The Williams sisters, Seles, Hewitt, to mention just a few, raised the level of their game by incorporating this shot into their arsenal. So, add the swinging volley into your game, and your opponent will know that you are determined to win...big time.

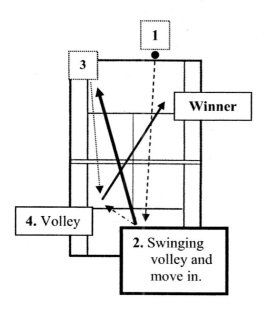

HIGH FOREHAND SWINGING VOLLEY *FRONT VIEW*

3. Early Prep. / 4. Step / 5. Contact   6. Follow Through
(1. Split Step / React / 2. Footwork)

HIGH FOREHAND SWINGING VOLLEY *SIDE VIEW*

3. Early Prep. / 4. Step   5. Point of Contact   6. Follow Through
(1. Split Step / React / 2. Footwork)

FOREHAND SWINGING VOLLEY *FRONT VIEW*

4. Step   5. Point of Contact   6. Follow Through
(1. Split Step / React / 2. Footwork / 3. Early Preparation)

FOREHAND SWINGING VOLLEY *SIDE VIEW*

2. Footwork   3. Early Preparation / 4. Step
(1. Split Step / React)

5. Point of Contact   6. Follow Through   7. Keep Moving

HIGH TWO-HANDED BACKHAND SWINGING VOLLEY

FRONT VIEW

4. Step   **5. Point of Contact**   **6. Follow Through**
(1. Split Step / React / 2. Footwork / 3. Early Preparation)

HIGH TWO-HANDED BACKHAND SWINGING VOLLEY

SIDE VIEW

4. Step   **5. Point of Contact**   **6. Follow Through**
(1. Split Step / React / 2. Footwork / 3. Early Preparation)

TWO-HANDED SWINGING VOLLEY *FRONT VIEW*

4. Step   **5. Point of Contact**   **6. Follow Through**
(1. Split Step / React / 2. Footwork / 3. Early Preparation)

TWO-HANDED SWINGING VOLLEY *SIDE VIEW*

3. Early Preparation   **4. Step**   **5. Point of Contact**
(1. Split Step / React / 2. Footwork)

6. Follow Through   **7. Keep Moving**

SWINGING VOLLEY

Forehand and Backhand

KEYS:
Perfect Timing
Balance
Firm Wrist

RECOMMENDED GRIPS:
Around waist level point of contact: Same grips used for forehand and backhand groundstrokes.[1]
High forehands and one-handed backhands: Continental.[1]

1. SPLIT STEP / REACT
- Get ready.[2]

2. FOOTWORK
- Eyes locked on the flying ball.
- Quickly move in position to hit the ball in the air (usually around the service line) at the ideal groundstroke striking zone or higher.

- Work the footwork like an approach shot.[2]

3. EARLY PREPARATION
- Compact backswing for control.
- Racquet head below the ball for topspin production.
- Free hand out in front (forehand).

> On high swinging volleys, drive the racquet end cap into the ball first; *then* the racquet head should impact the ball.

- On high shots, preparation is more like a regular volley but with a compact backswing.

4. STEP OUT IN FRONT

- Step out in front toward the target without stopping (weight transfer and forward momentum). Open stance swinging volleys are also very effective for around waist level shots due to the position of the hips during preparation, which allows you to hit through. Just make sure that the shoulders turn properly.[3]

- Body turns sideways maintaining good balance (coiling).
- No need for *deep* knee bends on waist level shots. Most of the power should be generated from the forward movement.
- Backswing should be compact to enhance control.[2]

- Keep head still throughout the stroke (keeping dynamic balance).
- **Forward motion** (for shots around waist level point of contact).
  - As racquet moves forward to the point of contact, knees extend up adding some power to the shot.
  - Hips and shoulders rotate forward into the flying ball. Make sure that the racquet head gets lower than the incoming ball before point of contact in order to generate topspin and good clearance over the net.
- **Forward motion** (for high shots).
  - Treat it like a regular volley, not much body and arm motion.
  - Drive the racquet end cap into the ball first and then the racquet head should impact the ball.

5. POINT OF CONTACT
- Eyes locked on the ball.

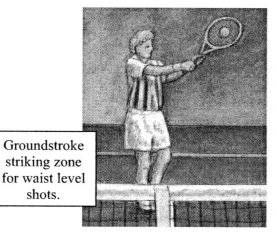

Groundstroke striking zone for waist level shots.

Head still.

- At point of contact, racquet face is square, brushing upward over the backside of the ball, imparting good topspin (waist level shots). Volley-like point of contact for high shots.
- Wrist firm.
- Weight fully transfers to the front foot. Front knee is extended. Back foot is on tiptoe or in the air (forward momentum).
- Keep head still throughout the shot.

6. FOLLOW THROUGH

- On high swinging volleys finish with a compact follow through, keeping the *elbows high*. On shots around the waist level finish with a full groundstroke-like follow through (racquet end cap looks forward to the target).
- Loose wrist.
- Following forward toward the target will help to better cover any possible return.

Finish with the elbows high.

Keep moving forward.

Head still.

Hit through the ball on high shots (high finish).

- On a high shot, make sure the racquet follows forward and *through the ball*, not down (keep elbow high).

7. KEEP MOVING

- Keep moving forward toward the target, following the flight of the ball, thereby covering any possible angles of return.

8. SPLIT STEP

- Get ready for the volley.

[1] See Chapter 1, **"Grips"**
[2] See Chapter 1, **"Anticipation & Footwork"**
[3] See Chapter 1, **"Stances"**

HALF VOLLEY

HALF VOLLEY

The "Don't Get Caught" Shot
and
The "Rhythm Changer"

The half volley is a creative, spontaneous shot used defensively when caught in "no man's land" on the way to the net. It can also be used offensively when it is played from anywhere on the court, but especially when playing inside or close behind the baseline, with the purpose of changing the opponent's rhythm (like shots hit on the rise or some returns of serve).

Every aggressive player (net rushers, "Serve & Volley" players) should master this shot, otherwise there will be a lot of pressure when charging the net for fear of returning a weak shot or making an unforced error.

This shot should be treated like a volley that cannot be hit out of the air. One-handed backhand players will have a much easier time reaching low half volleys. Therefore, two-handed players will need to release the top hand on the follow through in order to control the body balance and the stroke.

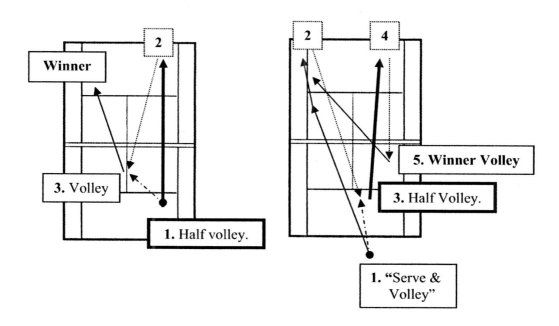

DEFENSIVE FOREHAND HALF VOLLEY *SIDE VIEW*

3. Compact Backswing   4. Step / Get Low
(1. Split Step / React / 2. Footwork)

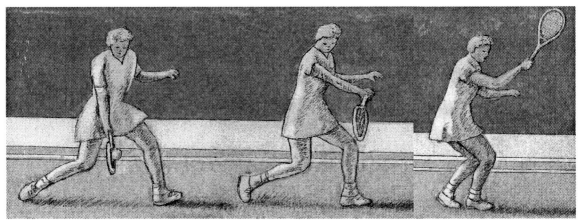

5. Point of Contact   6. Follow Through   7. Keep Moving

FOREHAND HALF VOLLEY *BACK VIEW*

4. Step / Get Low   5. Point of Contact
(1. Split Step / React / 2. Footwork / 3. Compact Backswing)

DEFENSIVE BACKHAND HALF VOLLEY *FRONT VIEW*

3. Backswing   4. Step / Get Low
(1. Split Step / React / 2. Footwork)

5. Point of Contact / 6. Follow Through

BACKHAND HALF VOLLEY *SIDE VIEW*

1. Split Step / React / 2. Footwork / 3. Backswing / 4. Step / Get Low

5. Point of Contact   6. Follow Through / 7. Keep Moving

HALF VOLLEY
DEFENSIVE (Low)

Forehand and Backhand

KEYS:
Get Low
Timing
Dynamic Balance

RECOMMENDED GRIPS:
Forehand and one-handed backhand: Continental.[2]
Two-handed backhand: (bottom/top hand) Continental/Eastern forehand, Continental/Semi-Western forehand.[2]

1. **SPLIT STEP / REACT**
   - Get ready.[3]
   - Racquet and elbows out in front of the body.

2. **FOOTWORK**
   - Get to the ball as quick as possible to reach to the volley (the half volley is an instinctive shot when not reaching the ball out of the air).

3. **PREPARATION**
   - Compact backswing.[4]

4. **STEP TOWARD THE BALL / GET LOW**

- Before contact, step forward as you get low by bending the knees. Step with the opposite foot of your racquet hand for the forehand and same foot as the hand that holds the racquet for the backhand. This step will help you to get closer and low to the ball, and it will also help you to get the shoulder a little sideways, placing your body in a more sound position.

5. POINT OF CONTACT

- Without stopping, but in dynamic balance (keep head still throughout the stroke), meet the ball out in front *right after* the bounce with the racquet face perpendicular or slightly open (depending on the depth of the shot required and height of the ball at contact). The racquet should get very low, almost touching the ground, as the rhythm of the point of contact is a quick "bounce-hit". Slow down the forward motion to maintain dynamic balance.
- Shoulders are sideways to control the placement (consistency) of the point of contact.
- Eyes locked on the ball.
- Wrist is firm, controlling the shot.
- Stay low and do not over-hit; let it happen (use placement and depth).

6. FOLLOW THROUGH

- Compact for a smooth continuous forward motion, necessary to reach a good position at the net.
- On two-handed (low) shots, release the top hand on the follow through in order to maintain dynamic balance as you continue moving forward.

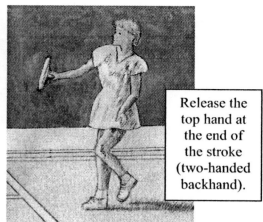

Release the top hand at the end of the stroke (two-handed backhand).

7. FOOTWORK

- Keep moving forward.

8. SPLIT STEP

- Get ready for the next shot (volley or lob).

HALF VOLLEY
OFFENSIVE

Forehand and Backhand

In today's game the offensive half volley is widely used due to the aggressive position the baseliners adopt during the rally (standing inside or close behind the baseline). With the purpose of changing the opponent's rhythm, aggressive players like Agassi, striking groundstrokes on the rise (hitting the ball as it comes up), mostly from inside the court, play half volleys from anywhere in the court, controlling the point and creating opportunities to attack.

Another good example of an offensive half volley is the return of serve. When your opponent's serve is fast and powerful, your reaction to return the serve should be quick and sharp, and the rhythm should be like the half volley (quick "bounce-hit").

It is played like a regular groundstroke with the difference of a compact backswing and a very fast forward swing. Topspin is the control factor of this aggressive shot, and, therefore, heavy spin is required. As mentioned before, it is most effective when it is hit from inside the baseline as an offensive groundstroke or as an approach shot to attack the net (hit the ball on the rise, as it comes up from the bounce).

[1] See Chapter 5, **"Different Players"**
[2] See Chapter 1, **"Grips"**
[3] See Chapter 1, **"Anticipation & Footwork"**
[4] See Chapter 1, **"Backswing Styles"**

SERVE & VOLLEY

SERVE & VOLLEY

The Surprise Attack

How many times have you gotten engaged in a long rally and wished you could finish the point quickly and easily. Sometimes your opponent is just in better physical shape, and because of that he controls the point. At other times perhaps his groundstrokes are more solid than yours, especially the crosscourt shots, thereby forcing you into a mistake or a low percentage shot. For any of these situations, the "Serve & Volley" game might be the answer.

There are other circumstances where the "Serve & Volley" game is useful also. You can use it anytime you need to change pace, disrupt the rhythm of your opponent, or when playing competitive doubles. It is also useful on fast surfaces like grass or carpet, when the bounce is uneven and quick (low). Attacking volleys right after a serve will definitely pay off.

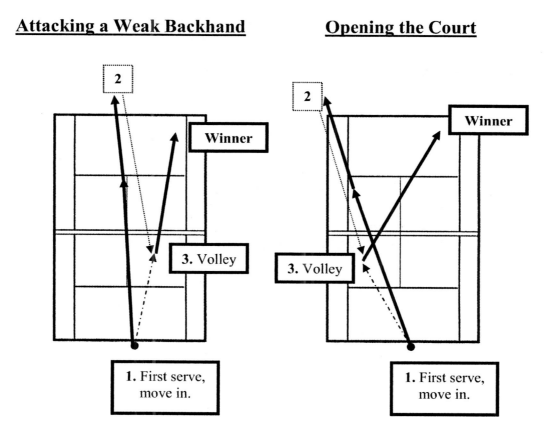

Attacking a Weak Backhand   **Opening the Court**

SERVE & VOLLEY *FRONT VIEW*

1. First Serve   2. Move In   3. Split Step

React   4. Volley   5. Recover

SERVE & VOLLEY *SIDE VIEW*

1. First Serve   **2. Move In**

3. Split / React / 4. Volley   **5. Recover**

SERVE & VOLLEY

KEYS:
First Serve
Split Step
Solid First Volley

RECOMMENDED GRIP:
Continental[1]

1. FIRST SERVE
- The effectiveness of the serve and volley attack will depend on the pressure and surprise of the first serve. A kick spin serve will give you more time to get closer to the net, while its high bounce will keep the returner pinned deep behind the baseline.[2]

2. FOOTWORK
- Move in quickly to get in position to volley (inside the service box).

3. SPLIT STEP / REACT
- Get ready for the volley.[3]

4. VOLLEY
- Use "First Volley" strategy.[4]

5. RECOVER / SPLIT STEP
- Get ready for the next shot (volley or lob).

---

[1] See Chapter 1, **"Grips"**
[2] See Chapter 1, **"Spins"**
[3] See Chapter 1, **"Anticipation & Footwork"**
[4] See Chapter 5, **"Volley Strategy"**

CHAPTER 4

SPECIALTY SHOTS

<u>LOB</u>

LOB

The Underrated Weapon

The lob, usually an underrated shot, can be one of the deadliest shots in the game. Once the ball is in the air, a well disguised high lob, offensive or defensive, can destroy your opponent's game plan or help you to recover and turn the tables on him (you'll become the aggressor by moving up to the net, while your opponent runs down the lob).

Many average players believe that the lob is just a shot to get out of trouble, sometimes, even a weakness, but advanced competitive players understand that it can be more than a defensive shot. An exceptional strategy is to bring the opponent to the net (with a drop shot) and then hit a lob over his head with topspin (offensive). Therefore, one of the most important aspects of the lob is when and how to execute it.

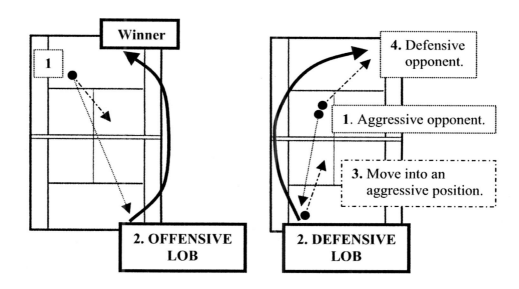

FOREHAND OFFENSIVE LOB *SIDE VIEW*

1. Split Step   **React**   **2. Disguise**

3. Forward Swing   **4. Contact**   **5. Follow Through**

ONE-HANDED BACKHAND OFFENSIVE LOB *FRONT VIEW*

2. Disguise
(1. Split Step / React)

3. Forward Swing

4. Point of Contact

5. Follow Through

6. Recovery

ONE-HANDED BACKHAND OFFENSIVE LOB *SIDE VIEW*

3. Forward Swing   4. Point of Contact   5. Follow Through
(1. Split Step / React / 2. Disguise)

TWO-HANDED BACKHAND OFFENSIVE LOB

2. Disguise   3. Forward Swing
(1. Split Step / React)

4. Contact   5. Follow Through

240

OFFENSIVE LOB
TOPSPIN

Forehand and Backhand

KEYS:
Disguise
Early Preparation
Apply Spin
Height and Depth

RECOMMENDED GRIPS:
Forehand and one-handed backhand: Eastern, Semi-Western forehand/backhand, Western forehand.[1]
Two-handed backhand: (bottom/top hand) Continental/Eastern forehand, Continental/Semi-Western forehand, Eastern backhand/ Eastern forehand, Eastern backhand/Semi-Western forehand.[1]

1. **SPLIT STEP / REACT**
    -   Get ready.

2. **DISGUISE**
    -   Make it look like a regular shot. **Footwork, early preparation** (backswing[2]), and all the ingredients of an effective groundstroke should be included.

3. **FORWARD SWING**
    -   Knees bend to get below the ball.
    -   **Weight Transfer**
        Step into the shot (weight shifts to the front foot).
    -   Racquet face should be pointing down and closed. This will help to brush the backside of the ball, imparting topspin.

4. POINT OF CONTACT

- Use a regular point of contact like any other topspin groundstroke, but instead of following forward right after the contact with your racquet aggressively brush up the backside of the ball and slightly under it. This vertical acceleration will impart heavy topspin and by hitting slightly under the ball will go high. Experiment with the angle of the racquet to develop a feel. The angle of the racquet face at point of contact will determine how high and deep the lob will be. Usually, the angle of the racquet face is almost perpendicular or just slightly open.

- Eyes locked on the ball.
- Weight fully transfers to the front foot.
- Front knee stays low to control the shot.

- Sometimes weight can not be transferred to the front foot at point of contact (under pressure), but still an aggressive topspin lob can be effectively produced (especially off the forehand side).

5. FOLLOW THROUGH

- Eyes steady at point of contact (striking zone) for a split second after the ball has left the strings (do not follow the ball with your eyes immediately after point of contact). This will help to control accuracy of the shot, as well as helping to maintain balance.
- Finish compact and high out in front of your body.
- Back foot on tiptoe to help maintain good balance.
- Loose wrist for more topspin and power (wrist snap).

Finish high.

A one-hand release sometimes is needed to lift the ball high.

Two-Handed Backhand

Free hand helps for balance.

One-Handed Backhand   **Forehand**

6. RECOVERY

- The back foot steps outside toward the sideline pushing the body to shuffle to the "Recovery Site". Open stance lobs have the advantage of having the outside foot ready to push back to the "Recovery Site", saving one step.[3]

FOREHAND DEFENSIVE LOB *FRONT VIEW*

1. Split Step / React / 2. Disguise   3. Forward Swing

4. Point of Contact   5. Follow Through

6. Recovery

FOREHAND DEFENSIVE LOB *SIDE VIEW*

1. Split Step   **React**   **2. Disguise / 3. Forward Swing**

4. Contact   **5. Follow Through / 6. Recovery**

BACKHAND DEFENSIVE LOB *SIDE VIEW*

3. Forward Swing   4. Point of Contact
(1. Split Step / React / 2. Disguise)

5. Follow Through

TWO-HANDED BACKHAND DEFENSIVE LOB *SIDE VIEW*

3. Forward Swing   **4. Point of Contact**
(1. Split Step / React / 2. Disguise)

5. Follow Through

DEFENSIVE LOB
UNDERSPIN

Forehand and Backhand

KEYS:
Disguise
Balance
Apply Spin
Height and Depth

RECOMMENDED GRIPS:
Forehand and one-handed backhand: Continental.[1]
Two-handed backhand: (bottom/top hand) Continental/Eastern forehand,
Continental/Semi-Western forehand.[1]

- Same procedures as with the topspin lob but it is disguised to look like a regular groundstroke slice.

| **Forehand** | **Two-Handed Backhand** | **One-Handed Backhand** |

- At point of contact the face of the racquet opens up, brushing the under part of the ball, imparting underspin.[4]
- This shot is a useful defensive tool for late shots hit off the back foot (weight back), against aggressive attacks (net rushers), or any situation where time to recover is needed.

- Follow the ball with the open racquet face, finishing high at shoulder level (one-handed backhand).

| Forehand | Two-Handed Backhand | One-Handed Backhand |

- Recover quickly to the "Recovery Site".[3]

[1] See Chapter 1, **"Grips"**
[2] See Chapter 1, **"Backswing Styles"**
[3] See Chapter 1, **"Anticipation & Footwork"**
[4] See Chapter 1, **"Spins"**

DROP SHOT

DROP SHOT

The Big Deceiver

The drop shot is a delicate, wise stroke played when your opponent is deep behind the baseline and you are well inside or when you want to bring him up to the net (move the opponent). With the element of surprise and well executed (with touch and feel), this shot will keep your opponent off balance every time you use it.

To maintain the element of surprise, you should not only disguise the shot (so it looks like a regular groundstroke), but use it selectively and sporadically. It is most effective when used on clay and grass courts. Also, use it when you are in control of the point, ahead in the game, or when you can take a little risk (not under pressure or when in trouble).

When the Opponent is Far
(Well Behind the Baseline)

Moving the Opponent

1

Winner

2. Drop shot.

1

Winner   **Winner**

3

4. Passing shot or lob.

2. Drop shot, and move in.

FOREHAND DROP SHOT *FRONT VIEW*

1. Split Step / React / 2. Footwork / 3. Early Preparation

Disguise   **4. Stop and Step**   **5. Point of Contact**

6. Compact Follow Through   **7. Recovery**

FOREHAND DROP SHOT *SIDE VIEW*

4. Stop and Step   5. Point of Contact
(1. Split Step / React / 2. Footwork / 3. Early Preparation / Disguise)

6. Follow Through   7. Recovery

TWO-HANDED BACKHAND DROP SHOT *FRONT VIEW*

Disguise   4. Stop and Step 5. Point of Contact
(1. Split Step / React / 2. Footwork / 3. Early Preparation)

6. Compact Follow Through

TWO-HANDED BACKHAND DROP SHOT *SIDE VIEW*

4. Stop and Step   **5. Point of Contact**
(1. Split Step / React / 2. Footwork / 3. Early Preparation / Disguise)

6. Compact Follow Through

BACKHAND DROP SHOT *FRONT VIEW*

4. Stop and Step   **5. Point of Contact**
(1. Split Step / React / 2. Footwork / 3. Early Preparation / Disguise)

6. Compact Follow Through

BACKHAND DROP SHOT *SIDE VIEW*

4. Stop and Step   5. Point of Contact
(1. Split Step / React / 2. Footwork / 3. Early Preparation / Disguise)

6. Compact Follow Through

DROP SHOT

Forehand and Backhand

KEYS:
Disguise
Balance
Loose Wrist
Selective Use[1]

RECOMMENDED GRIPS:
Forehand: Continental, Eastern.[2]
One-handed backhand: Continental.[2]
Two-handed backhand: (bottom/top hand) Continental/Eastern forehand, Continental/Semi-Western forehand, Eastern forehand/ Eastern forehand, Eastern forehand/Semi-Western forehand.[2]

1. **SPLIT STEP / REACT**
   - Get ready.[3]

2. **FOOTWORK**
   - Get to the ball early.[3]

3. **EARLY PREPARATION / DISGUISE**
   - Shoulder turn, racquet back[4], and weight transfer should be exactly like any other regular groundstroke (forehand, backhand, topspin or slice), so your opponent won't be able to anticipate the drop shot (complete surprise).
   - Racquet forward motion should be held until the last second, so that, when it is executed, it will be too late for your opponent to reach it.

Drop Shot Disguise   **Slice Backhand**

4. STOP AND STEP OUT IN FRONT

A. Stop and Step
- Stop your body's forward motion so the drop shot stays short.
- Step out in front to insure a controlled point of contact. If an open stance shot is played,[5] make sure shoulders are slightly sideways.

B. Knees Bend
- Knees slightly bent for control and to adjust to the height of the ball.

C. Head Control
- Head stays steady throughout the stroke.

D. Eye Control
- Eyes should be locked on the ball. A common mistake is to look forward to the intended target just before point of contact.

E. Forward Momentum
- Because the drop shot does not require any power, the racquet is held until the last second, stopping most of the body's forward momentum (impulse).

F. Knees Extension
- Stay fairly low to keep control. Extending your knees will add unnecessary power to the shot.

❖ *JUST BEFORE* POINT OF CONTACT
- Adjust the disguised backswing (if necessary) for the drop shot with a compact and quick motion.
- Because extreme underspin must be imparted on the ball, racquet head has to be above the ball.[6]
- Loose wrist (spin production and power absorption).

5. POINT OF CONTACT

- Eyes locked on the ball.
- Loose wrist.
- Contact the ball out in front.
- Brush the backside and under the ball with a slight open racquet face.[3] Wrist remains loose to create spin and to absorb power.
- There should be no creation of power, only control with spin. To do that, the knees remain slightly bent, shoulder rotation and weight shifting forward is minimal.

Free hand helps to keep the balance.

- Keep head still throughout the shot.

- On the one-handed backhand shot, the free hand remains behind, helping to maintain balance.

6. FOLLOW THROUGH

- Eyes steady at point of contact (striking zone) for a split second after the ball has left the strings (do not follow the ball with your eyes immediately after point of contact). This will help to control accuracy of the shot, as well as maintain balance.
- There is practically no follow through. Instead, the racquet continues on a downward path.
- Wrist remains loose.

7. RECOVERY

- The ball should clear the net and die right over it, out of reach of your opponent. The point should be over. However, as in any other situation, always be ready for another shot. In this case, move in to the net, especially if your opponent runs the ball down.

 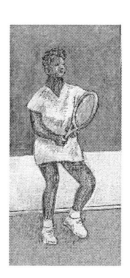

[1] See Chapter 5, **"Drop Shot Strategy"**
[2] See Chapter 1, **"Grips"**
[3] See Chapter 1, **"Anticipation & Footwork"**
[4] See Chapter 1, **"Backswing Styles"**
[5] See Chapter 1, **"Stances"**
[6] See Chapter 1, **"Spins"**

PASSING SHOT

PASSING SHOT

The "Go-for-It" Shot

The passing shot is like any regular forehand or backhand but with a different attitude. Since it is a shot produced under pressure (opponent is at or coming up to the net), the passing shot sometimes may require you to shorten the backswing and follow through (depending on your opponent's approach shot), making it more compact for a quicker response. However, the major difference between it and a regular groundstroke is its attitude. The passing shot is really a "go-for-it" shot. You want to be positive, with no hesitation, and pinpoint the shot with authority to at least force your opponent to volley weakly if you do not hit an outright winner.

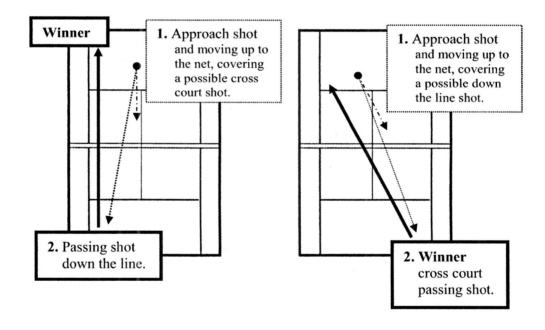

Winner

1. Approach shot and moving up to the net, covering a possible cross court shot.

2. Passing shot down the line.

1. Approach shot and moving up to the net, covering a possible down the line shot.

2. **Winner** cross court passing shot.

RUNNING FOREHAND PASSING SHOT *FRONT VIEW*
(Down the Line, Off the Front Foot)

1. Split Step / React / 2. Footwork

3. Good Preparation   **4. Step / 5. Point of Contact**

6. Follow Through   **7. Recovery**

RUNNING FOREHAND PASSING SHOT *FRONT VIEW*
(Crosscourt, Off the Back Foot)

2. Footwork
(1. Split Step / React)

3. Good Preparation   **(4. Step) / 5. Contact**

6. Follow Through

7. Recovery

RUNNING FOREHAND PASSING SHOT *SIDE VIEW*
(Crosscourt, Off the Back Foot)

2. Footwork
(1. Split Step / React)

3. Good Preparation

4. (Step) / 5. Contact　　**6. Follow Through**　　**7. Recovery**

ONE-HANDED BACKHAND PASSING SHOT *FRONT VIEW*

3. Good Preparation   **4. Stop and Step**   **5. Point of Contact**
(1. Split Step / React / 2. Footwork)

6. Follow Through   **7. Recovery**

ONE-HANDED BACKHAND PASSING SHOT *FRONT VIEW*

2. Footwork
(1. Split Step / React)   **3. Good Preparation**

4. Step / 5. Point of Contact   6. Follow Through   7. Recovery

PASSING SHOT
FLAT OR TOPSPIN

Forehand and Backhand

KEYS:
Decisiveness
Balance
Low Shot

RECOMMENDED GRIPS:
Same grips used for topspin forehand and backhand groundstrokes.[1]

1. **SPLIT STEP / REACT**
   - Get ready (anticipate the shot if possible).[2]

2. **FOOTWORK**
   - Get to the ball as early as possible.[2]

3. **GOOD PREPARATION**
   - Includes all elements of a drive forehand and backhand with the exception that it sometimes requires a shorter backswing[3] to compensate for the pressure (lack of time) that you opponent is putting upon you.

4. STOP AND STEP OUT IN FRONT

- **Stop and Step**

  Stop to hit a controlled, balanced shot and step out in front toward the target. On running shots (forehand and backhand), hit through without stopping off the front foot, so the back foot, subsequently, stops the body's inertia and helps you to recover. On the forehand side, when the point of contact is late or behind, hitting off the back foot it is still very effective, especially aiming down the line.[2] Though it can be hit from an open stance,[4] a step forward will guarantee good weight transfer into the ball, therefore, good power production.

- **Head Control**

  One of the essential elements of this stroke is good balance. By keeping the head still throughout the stroke, balance will be maintained, especially on running shots when there is no time to stop.

- **Eye Control**

  Eyes should be locked on the ball. One common mistake is to watch the opponent as he moves forward attacking the net and, therefore, losing track of the ball.

5. POINT OF CONTACT

- Eyes locked on the ball.
- Racquet square, (face perpendicular to ground and racquet horizontal) and out in front of the front knee at waist level (striking zone). On running shots, the shoulders might stay sideways because of the running position (closed stance).[4]

- Wrist firm.
- Weight fully transfered to front foot.
- Keep head still throughout the shot.

6. FOLLOW THROUGH

- Sometimes, for more control, a shorter follow through is required in order to pinpoint the shot.
- Finish high on running shots (forehand and backhand), compensating for the lack of shoulder rotation.

Head still.

7. RECOVERY

- Recover by moving forward and diagonally (or following the direction of your passing shot), to return any possible volley from your opponent.[5]

[1] See Chapter 1, **"Grips"**
[2] See Chapter 1, **"Anticipation & Footwork"**
[3] See Chapter 1, **"Backswing Styles"**
[4] See Chapter 1, **"Stances"**
[5] See Chapter 5, **"Passing Shot Strategy"**

ANGLE SHOT

ANGLE SHOT

The Unreachable

Though not widely used because of its high degree of difficulty, the angle shots are a great way of opening up the court, pass a net rusher, or finishing a point. *Aggressive* sharp angle shots must have a heavy topspin load and *touch* sharp angle shots need marked underspin (almost like a drop shot). Otherwise, the ball will not stay in the court.

This shot leaves you in a weak position in the court even if you recover quickly. Therefore, you must make sure that you force your opponent to get to it or make a clean winner.

An aggressive angle shot is a tough shot to make, especially for one-handed backhand players, but it is definitely a tough shot to return.

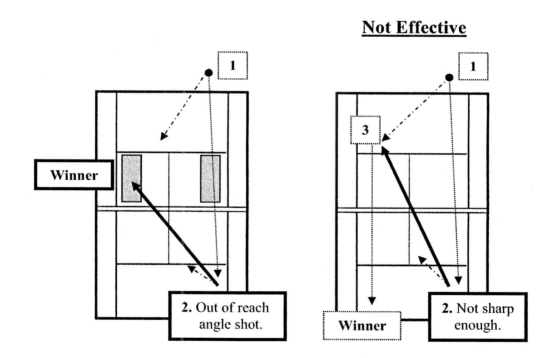

Not Effective

FOREHAND UNDERSPIN TOUCH ANGLE SHOT

SIDE VIEW

2. Footwork   **3. Early Preparation / 4. Slow Down**
(1. Split Step / React)

5. Point of Contact   **6. Follow Through / 7. Recovery**

TWO-HANDED BACKHAND TOPSPIN ANGLE SHOT

FRONT VIEW

5. Point of Contact   6. Follow Through   7. Recovery
(1. Split Step / React / 2. Footwork / 3. Early Preparation / 4. Slow Down)

SIDE VIEW

5. Point of Contact   6. Follow Through   7. Recovery
(1. Split Step / React / 2. Footwork / 3. Early Preparation / 4. Slow Down)

ANGLE SHOT
UNDERSPIN OR TOPSPIN

Forehand and Backhand

KEYS:
Balance
Heavy Spin
Placement

RECOMMENDED GRIPS:
Same grips used for topspin forehand and backhand groundstrokes.[1]

1. SPLIT STEP / REACT
- Get ready (anticipate a short ball if possible).[2]

2. FOOTWORK
- Get to the ball early.[2]

3. EARLY PREPARATION
A. Shoulder turn, racquet back[3], and weight transfer should be just like any other regular stroke (forehand, backhand, topspin, or underspin).
B. Knees bend to adjust to the height of the ball (control).

A completely disguised shot. At this point it looks like a regular underspin slice shot with no signs of placement.

4. STOP OR SLOW DOWN

A. Stop or Slow Down

- Stop or slow down your forward momentum to enhance control.
- A square stance can be used, but open stance[4] will help to place the ball easier in a sharp angle.

B. Head Control

- Head stays steady throughout the stroke.

C. Eye Control

- Eyes should be locked on the ball. A common mistake is to look forward to the intended target just before the point of contact.

D. Knees Extension

- Stay low to keep control. Extending your knees will add unnecessary power to the shot.

E. Forward Momentum

- Because the focus is on spin (placement of the ball), most of the action (acceleration) is in the brushing upon the back (or outside) of the ball (upward for topspin, downward for underspin).[5]

5. POINT OF CONTACT

- Eyes locked on the ball.
- Wrist loose (helps creation of an angle and spin).
- Contact the ball out in front with the racquet face angled.
- Brush the outside of the ball accordingly for topspin or underspin.
- There should be no creation of power, only control with spin. To do that the knees remain slightly bent, and shoulder rotation and weight shifting is minimal.

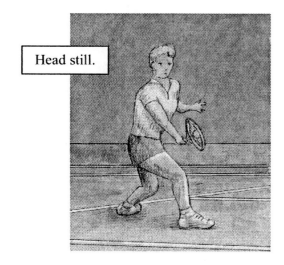

Head still.

6. FOLLOW THROUGH

- Wrist remains loose (slows down the ball).
- Follow through is slightly shorter than a normal stroke (maximizing placement, not power).

7. RECOVERY

- The ball should be placed far enough from your opponent, forcing him to hit a weak shot if you do not hit an outright clean winner. As in any other situation, always be ready for another shot, especially if your opponent runs down the ball.

[1] See Chapter 1, **"Grips"**
[2] See Chapter 1, **"Anticipation & Footwork"**
[3] See Chapter 1, **"Backswing Styles"**
[4] See Chapter 1, **"Stances"**
[5] See Chapter 1, **"Spins"**

CHAPTER 5

STRATEGY

STRATEGY

BASIC STROKES

GROUNDSTROKES

STRATEGY: PLAYING THE GAME

Basic Strategy, Winning Patterns and Percentage Tennis

GENERAL RULE:

KEEP THE BALL IN THE COURT

- Hit the ball as hard as you can, as long as you can keep it in the court, for the duration of the point. You must find the limit of your power (how hard you can hit) before losing control of the ball.
- Control is the key to consistency, and spin will be the means to achieve it.[1]
- Once you can keep the ball in play consistently (long rallies), you'll need to be able to direct the ball and follow a high percentage winning pattern (strategy) and/or follow a specific plan (tactic) to exploit your opponent's weaknesses.

Keeping the Ball in Play

- Play within the gray box (mostly with topspin), leaving a safety path of 3 feet around it, to achieve fewer unforced errors, greater continuity of shots, and, thereby, keeping the ball in the court.

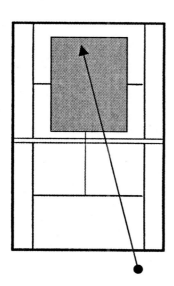

Shot Selection

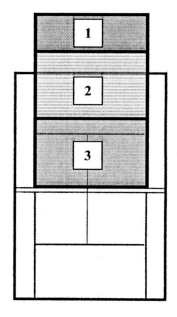

Tennis is about situations and executions. The best tennis happens when it is played on automatic pilot. In order to achieve this, use an automatic shot selection according to the situation. Remember, there is no right or wrong. Each situation can have several variables, so it is a matter of judgment, position and opportunity.

1. If you are in this box (**1**) just before making contact, play *defensive shots* (usually high and deep).
2. If you are in this box (**2**) just before making contact, play *percentage shots* (build up the point and create an opportunity to finish the point).
3. If you are in this box (**3**) just before making contact, play *offensive shots*, which include: transitional shots, volleys, and overheads (finish the point).

GROUNDSTROKES: Forehand and Backhand

1. KEEP THE BALL CROSSCOURT

*   Do you ever wonder why professionals keep crosscourt rallies longer than any other kind of rallies? They know that the first one who changes direction takes a greater risk by hitting a lower percentage shot (i.e. down the line). That is why the player who has more consistent crosscourt shots will probably end up winning the game.

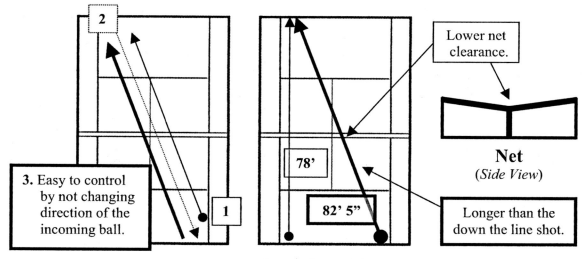

Easy to Control   **Length and Height of the Shot**

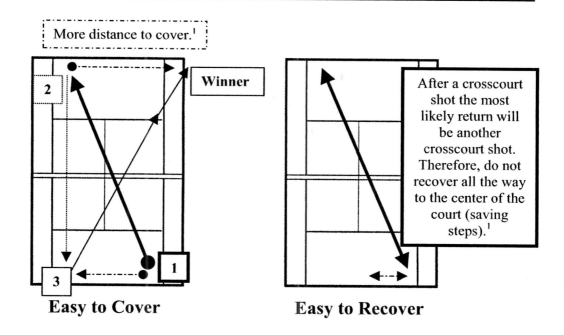

Easy to Cover

Easy to Recover

More distance to cover.[1]

Winner

After a crosscourt shot the most likely return will be another crosscourt shot. Therefore, do not recover all the way to the center of the court (saving steps).[1]

2. WHEN TO HIT DOWN THE LINE
- Hit down the line mostly for attacking shots.
- On short balls, like approach shots, follow to the net.
- After sharp angle shots, hit outside in, behind the player.

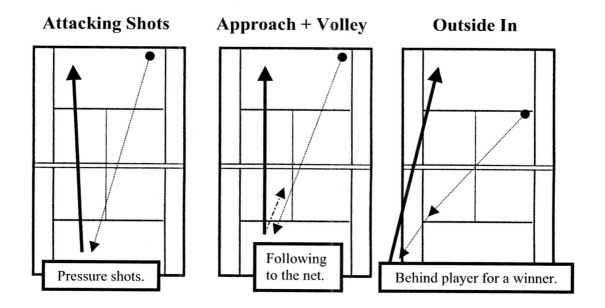

Attacking Shots

Approach + Volley

Outside In

Pressure shots.

Following to the net.

Behind player for a winner.

3. HIT DEEP

- If you lose your rhythm or timing and find yourself missing shots, get out of trouble by hitting deep (and high). Your opponent will not be able to attack, and this will give you enough hitting time to get back into rhythm. For players who move well side to side, hit deep and right at the body.

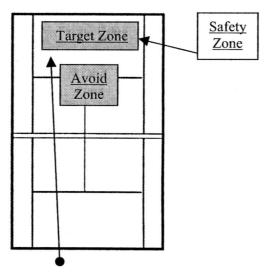

4. USE YOUR STRENGTH (Exploit Opponent's Weaknesses)

- For most of the players, a forehand is not just a shot but a weapon. This shot, when used properly, can open up the court or force a weak return. One good example is running around the backhand and hitting an inside-out shot. Your strength might be some other shot. Find it and use it wisely.

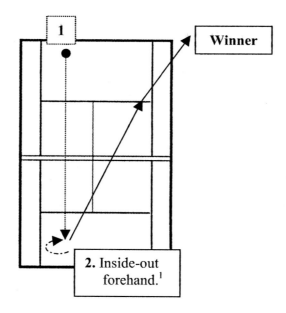

- Change strategy when your opponent's weakness is stronger than your weakness.

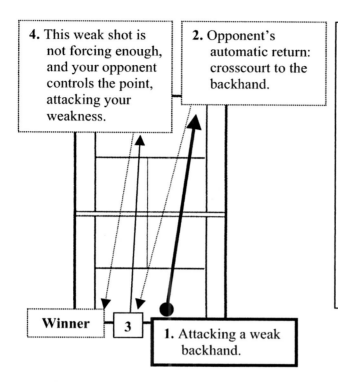

4. This weak shot is not forcing enough, and your opponent controls the point, attacking your weakness.

2. Opponent's automatic return: crosscourt to the backhand.

Be aware when you attack a weakness. Make sure that your opponent's return is not an automatic shot to your weakness, especially if your weakness is weaker than your opponent's. This situation will create an advantage in his favor and make it very difficult for you to follow your plan. The example shown to the left is one of many combinations, which depends on your and your opponent's shot-making abilities.

Winner | 3 | **1.** Attacking a weak backhand.

5. MOVE YOUR OPPONENT

- Move your opponent side to side, forcing him into a defensive game (also opening the court for angle shots).
- Wrong footing your opponent by hitting behind him (especially on clay courts, where changing directions is most difficult).

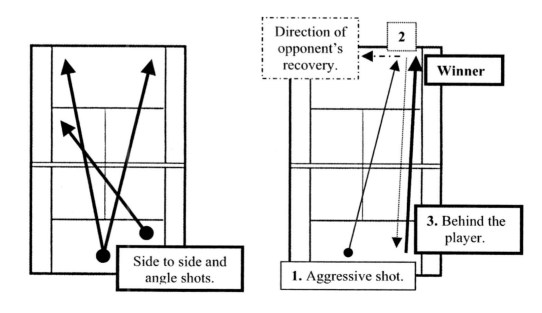

Side to side and angle shots.

Direction of opponent's recovery.

2

Winner

3. Behind the player.

1. Aggressive shot.

6. FORCING GROUNDSTROKES: Attacking Game
(Imposing a Weak Return by Utilizing your Strength and Strategy)

- **Powerful shots** (hard and heavy spin). To be used in conjunction with a well-rounded tactical plan, especially to a weakness, forcing a mistake or a weak return to open up the court or go for a winner.
- **Tactical shots**. Be smart on the court and exploit your opponent's weaknesses, maximizing you strength. Use ball placement, spin, and power to win the important points.[1]
- **Pressure shots**. By keeping the pressure with high percentage tennis and depth throughout the rally (also by charging the net), you can make your opponent become impatient, and he may go for difficult or low percentage shots.
- **Hitting early**. By stepping inside the baseline and making contact early (at peak of the bounce), cutting off time for your opponent to react.

MAJOR POINTS TO CONSIDER

- To win you do not necessarily need better strokes than your opponent. Play percentage tennis and always follow a good strategic plan, maximizing your strength and attacking your opponent's weaknesses.
- Be flexible enough to change your game plan in order to adapt to your opponent's counter-attack (momentum shifts).
- *Good shot selection*: know your limitations. Do not attack when you are out of position. When under pressure, return the shot deep to a weakness (lob or looping shot), regain good position in the court, and return to your plan.
- If your opponent hits hard, powerful, deep groundstrokes move back a little (to gain time), but if he hits a lot of angle shots, you should move inside the baseline in order to cut off the angle of the shot more easily.
- In difficult moments always analyze the situation and reach a decision for the next strategy.
- Keep unforced errors to a minimum by not changing the direction of the incoming ball (when you are under pressure, return shots to the same location that the ball came from).
- Apply good topspin on baseline rallies, and aim 3 feet inside the lines.
- Keep the pressure on by following the serve with an aggressive forcing shot (first shot right after the serve).

VOLLEY

1. FIRST VOLLEY (After the approach shot or any transitional shot.)

- Do not try to win this shot. This volley is a difficult one (far from net, out of position), and should be treated as a *set up shot*.

- As your opponent is about to return your transitional shot, you should be at the "Ideal Split Area" (ISA) doing a split step.[2] With a split at the right time (right before your opponent contacts the ball), you should be able to reach the first volley. Then keep moving forward to the "Ideal Volley Area" (IVA), split again to place a more effective volley, maybe even a winner (closer to the net).

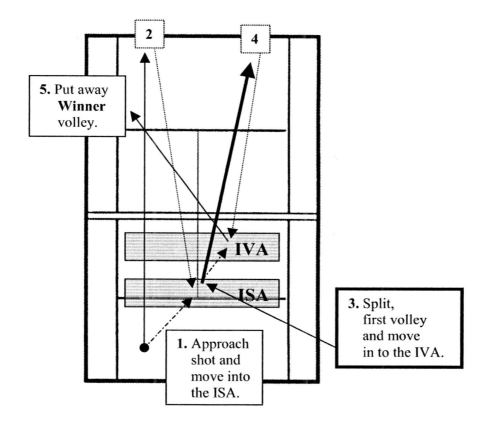

- There are endless combinations between the first volley and subsequent volleys (put away shots), but placing the first volley deep and straight ahead (of your position), will not create a sharp angle, and therefore, will make it much easier to cover the net (check also "High and Low" volleys).

- Do not get too close to the net, otherwise, any lob will become unreachable.

- Notice that after the split step you should move *diagonally* forward.[2] This way, as you move to the ball, you get closer to the net, cutting off the angle of any possible shot. By doing this, you gain angle production for your volley, you attack the ball aggressively, and you shorten the reaction time of your opponent.

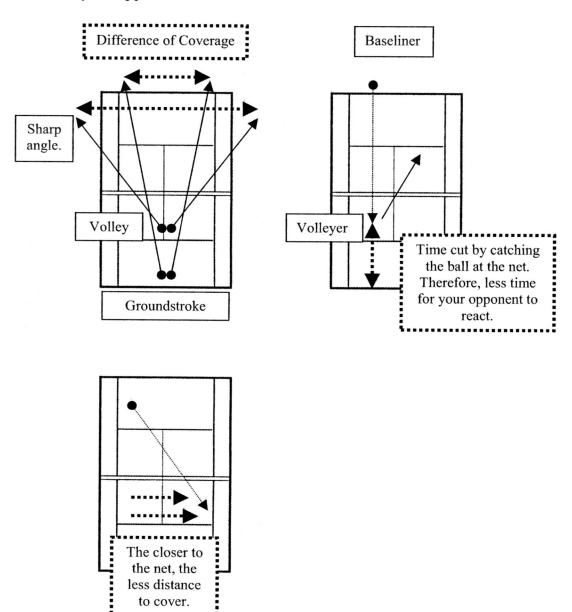

Where to Stand Once You Get to the "Ideal Volley Area" (IVA)

- Always stay in front of your opponent's eyes, wherever he is on the court (at the baseline or coming up to the net, covering any possible angle).

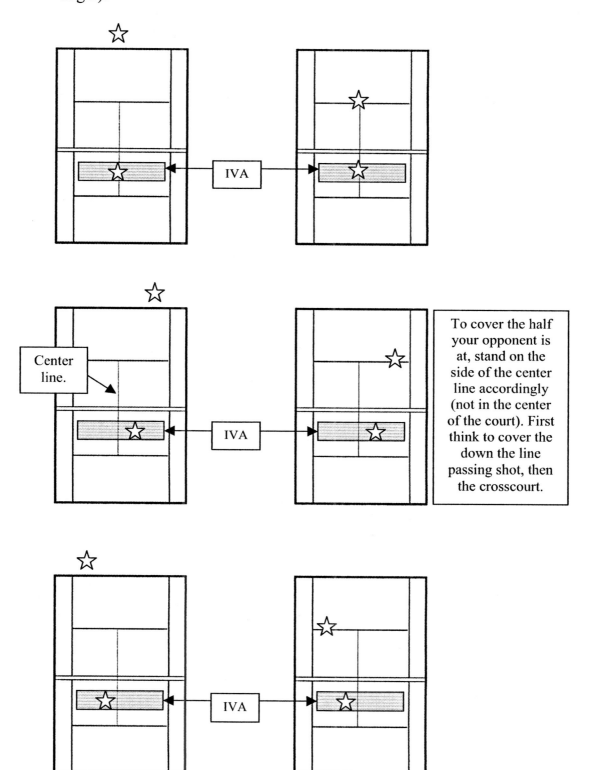

To cover the half your opponent is at, stand on the side of the center line accordingly (not in the center of the court). First think to cover the down the line passing shot, then the crosscourt.

2. LOW VOLLEY

- On low volleys or when volleying close to the sideline, aim *deep* down the line. This way, by not creating an angle, it will be easier to cover the next volley. Also, when volleying a low shot, you will need to open slightly the face of the racquet (how much will depend on your position relative to the net and how deep you need the shot to be), which will produce a higher bouncing shot. If this volley lands short, your opponent will move up, attacking you and putting away the easy shot. Hitting that low shot crosscourt instead will open up the court creating too much net to cover.

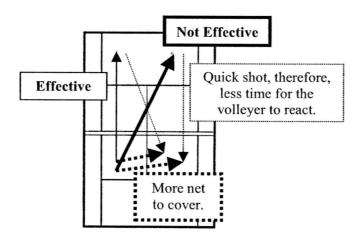

3. HIGH VOLLEY

- On high volleys, when at the "Ideal Volley Area", hit crosscourt or away from the player for an aggressive shot or winner put away.

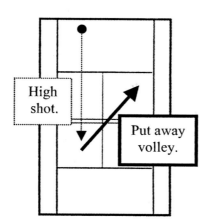

SERVE

1. PLACING THE FIRST SERVE into the Forehand

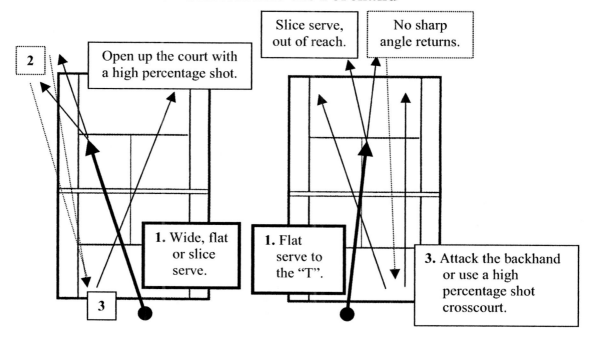

Slice serve, out of reach.

No sharp angle returns.

Open up the court with a high percentage shot.

1. Wide, flat or slice serve.

1. Flat serve to the "T".

3. Attack the backhand or use a high percentage shot crosscourt.

PLACING THE FIRST SERVE into the Backhand

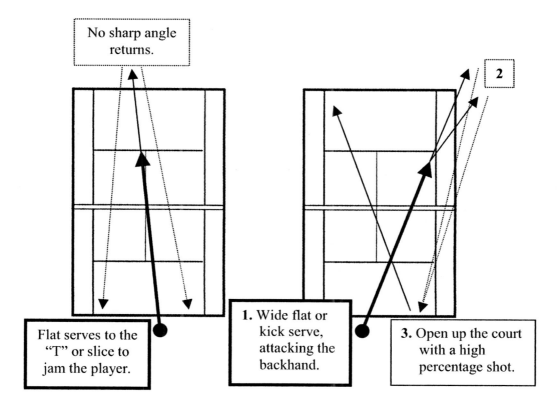

No sharp angle returns.

Flat serves to the "T" or slice to jam the player.

1. Wide flat or kick serve, attacking the backhand.

3. Open up the court with a high percentage shot.

2. PLACING THE SECOND SERVE

Same strategy as that of the first serve, but:

- Use more spin and kick serves for higher percentage shots.[3]
- Attack a weakness.
- Mix up the serves (placement and spin) to keep your opponent guessing, so your opponent will not have the chance to attack a weaker second serve.
- Aim deep, but not as deep as a first serve.
- If second serve is weak, make sure you get more first serves in, taking some pace off and replacing it with spin (higher percentage serve).

SERVE VARIATIONS (First and Second)

Right to the Body

Usually flat, but most effective when mixed up with different spins.

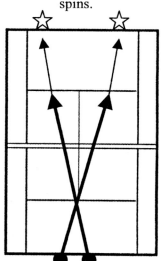

Wide Angle

Usually shorter, with slice to the deuce court and topspin to the ad court.

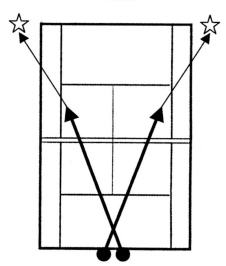

SERVER'S GOALS

Hold the Service Game

- Get between 60 to 70 percent of first serves in.
- Get the first serve in on important points.[2]
- Impose an offensive (aggressive) game in order to follow the strategy planned (disregarding player's game style). Also, force for a weak return so you can start the attack right from the first shot after the serve.

RETURN OF SERVE

- Depth and placement should be the focus, not power.
- For fast serves, use a block style return. If possible, depending on reaction time, serve speed, and spin, apply some topspin.
- On weak serves, attack the ball and follow to the net.
- For placement, think strategy: your strength against his weakness.

1. WHERE TO STAND FOR A *FIRST* SERVE

- If the serve is fast and deep, stand about 1 to 3 feet behind the baseline to gain some time and produce a solid return. Also consider shortening up the backswing and holding the racquet an inch or two shorter (especially for long body racquets) to be able to maneuver more quickly.
- If the serve is usually wide, especially with slice, stand closer to the baseline to cut down the angle of the serve and move diagonally to the ball.[2]
- Consider all variables: spins, depth, wind and surface of the court.

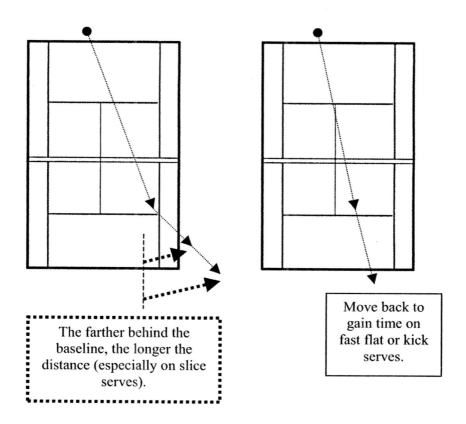

The farther behind the baseline, the longer the distance (especially on slice serves).

Move back to gain time on fast flat or kick serves.

2. WHERE TO STAND FOR A *WEAK OR SECOND* SERVE

- If the serve is weak, move inside the baseline. Consider the "Chip & Charge" strategy.
- For second serves stand closer to the baseline to keep up the pressure on the server and to get ready to attack the shorter serve.

3. RETURNING A *WIDE* SERVE

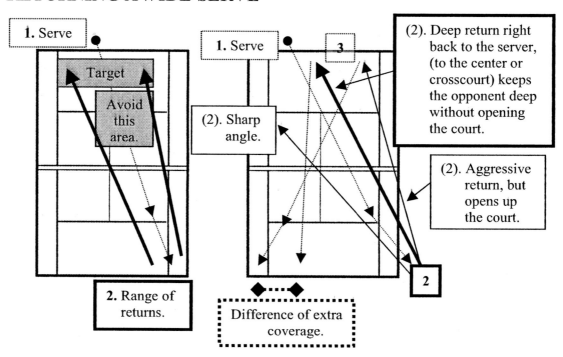

4. RETURNING A *DOWN THE T* SERVE

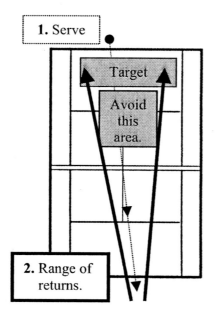

5. RETURNING A *"RIGHT TO THE BODY"* SERVE

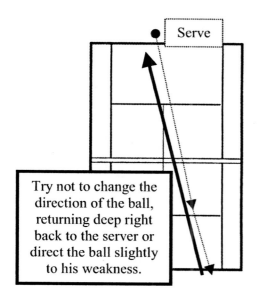

Serve

Try not to change the direction of the ball, returning deep right back to the server or direct the ball slightly to his weakness.

6. RETURNING A *"SERVE & VOLLEY"* PLAYER
- **When the Serve is *Wide***

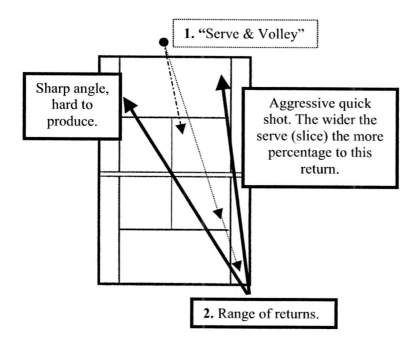

1. "Serve & Volley"

Sharp angle, hard to produce.

Aggressive quick shot. The wider the serve (slice) the more percentage to this return.

2. Range of returns.

• **When the Serve is *Down the "T"***

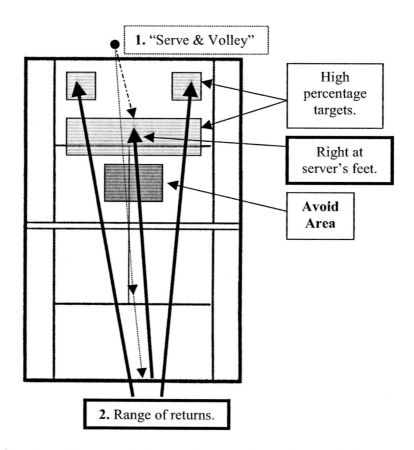

1. "Serve & Volley"

High percentage targets.

Right at server's feet.

Avoid Area

2. Range of returns.

7. RETURNING AND ATTACKING THE NET ("Chip & Charge")
(Shallow and Second Serves)

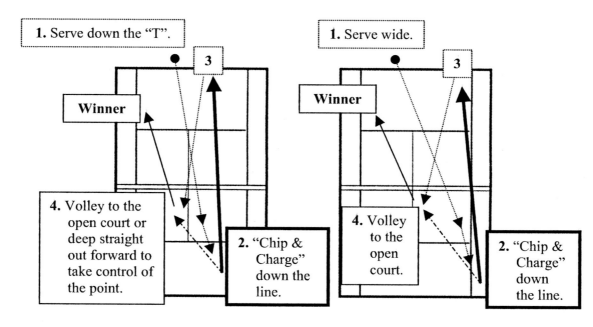

1. Serve down the "T".

3

Winner

4. Volley to the open court or deep straight out forward to take control of the point.

2. "Chip & Charge" down the line.

1. Serve wide.

3

Winner

4. Volley to the open court.

2. "Chip & Charge" down the line.

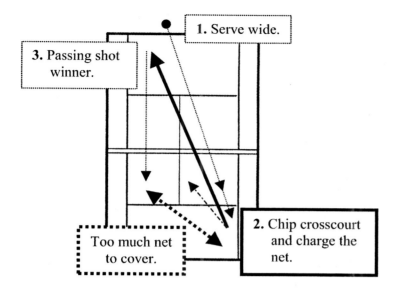

- Returning crosscourt when charging the net leaves too much net to cover (low percentage). If the plan is attacking a weak forehand or backhand, the crosscourt could be the right choice, but for most cases a better shot would be deep down the center towards the weak side, reducing the distance between you and the next possible shot.

RETURNER'S GOALS

Break Service Game

- Anticipate the serve by watching the toss position, spin and racquet face at point of contact.[3]
- Return the ball at all costs, regardless of how strong your opponent's serve is.
- Impose your game, aiming deep to a weakness or by using a specific pattern of play, forcing the server to make a weak shot.
- Get to the net ("Chip & Charge") whenever possible.

Note: When not mentioned, examples for the deuce court (forehand) will be identical for the ad court (backhand).

OVERHEAD

- When the overhead is hit off the center of the court, the most effective target is the opposite area close to the intersection of the service line and the singles sideline because this produces the most pronounced angle, which makes it impossible to return. It is a harder target to hit, so a deep shot to the open court will also do the job.

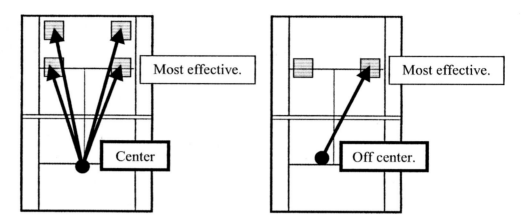

- Always try to hit overheads without the bounce, rather than letting the ball bounce (cuts off the opponent's time to recover). Also if you let it bounce, the angle of incidence will make this bouncing overhead difficult to hit, moving you further back away from the net and reducing your aggressive position.
- Let the ball bounce on very high lobs. Those super high lobs are tough to judge and the angle of incidence will not be an issue.

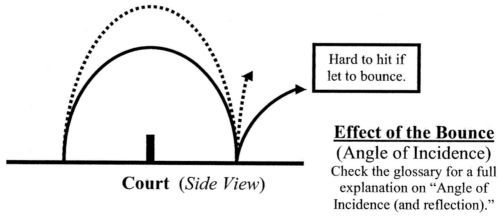

Court *(Side View)*

Effect of the Bounce
(Angle of Incidence)
Check the glossary for a full explanation on "Angle of Incidence (and reflection)."

[1] See Chapter 1, **"Anticipation & Footwork"**
[2] See Chapter 6, **"While Playing the Match"**
[3] See Chapter 1, **"Spins"**

STRATEGY

TRANSITIONAL GAME

APPROACH SHOT

HALF VOLLEY

TRANSITIONAL SHOTS:

APPROACH SHOT, SWINGING VOLLEY, HALF VOLLEY

- The weaker you are as a volleyer *or* the greater you opponent's passing shots are, the better your transitional shots ought to be.

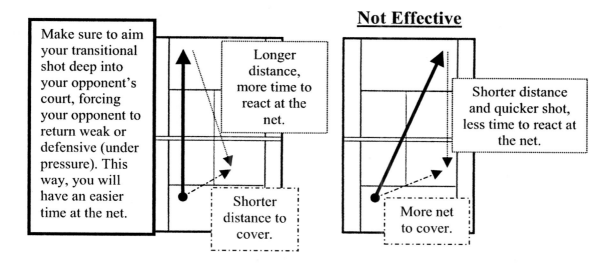

- *Note*: A short transitional shot will leave too much time for your opponent to react and attack you (you might still be in a vulnerable position), and therefore, finding a way to pass you.
- **Range of Motion**
  Aiming the approach shot *straight ahead* of your position in the court (down the line for off center shots), will lead you into a much easier position to cover any possible passing shot from your opponent.

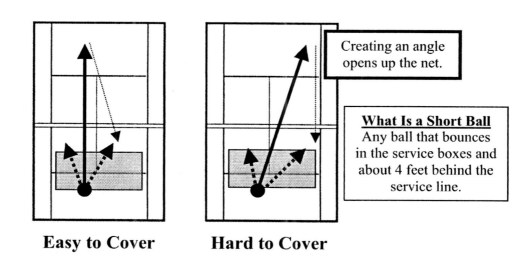

Easy to Cover   **Hard to Cover**

SERVE & VOLLEY

1. FIRST SERVE

- A forcing serve is a must. With a second serve the surprise effect and psychological factor will not be as effective as with the first serve.
- Deep kick serves will give more time to reach the net and will keep your opponent behind the baseline due to the high bounce.
- Place serve tactically, exploiting the opponent's weaknesses.

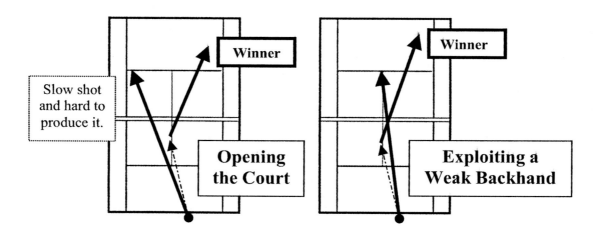

2. FIRST VOLLEY
Covering the Net

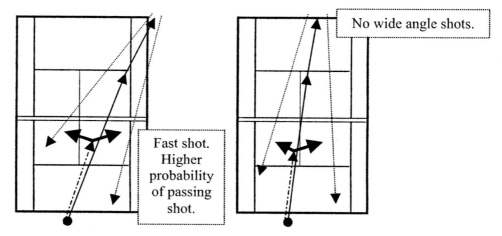

- Placement of the first volley depends on the serve placement and quality of the opponent's return. Sometimes your best volley is to the open court (make him move) or behind your opponent (opposite to his motion). However, most importantly, keep the opponent guessing.

STRATEGY

SPECIALTY SHOTS

LOB

- Defensive or offensive, the lob is not an easy shot to perform. Take into consideration the height of the player, his ability to move, the quality of his overheads, the sun and wind conditions.

- Usually it is played high to the backhand side, so the opponent will have a hard time returning a high bouncing backhand shot (it is much harder than a high forehand shot), and crosscourt, because the court is longer (higher percentage shot).

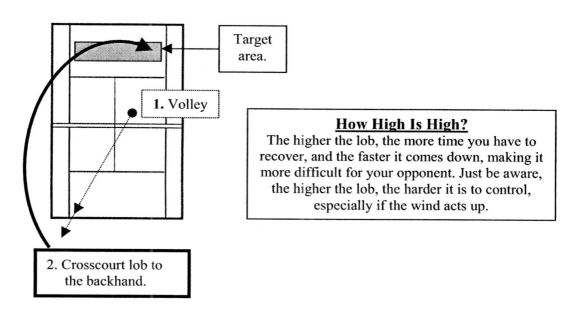

Target area.

1. Volley

2. Crosscourt lob to the backhand.

> ### How High Is High?
> The higher the lob, the more time you have to recover, and the faster it comes down, making it more difficult for your opponent. Just be aware, the higher the lob, the harder it is to control, especially if the wind acts up.

WHEN TO USE THE LOB
Defensive and Offensive

- In pressure situations (deep behind baseline and under aggressive attack) and when time to recover is required (regaining court positioning).
- Physical tiredness and to slow down the pace of the point.
- Against a good volleyer.
- Against a volleyer who gets too close to the net (between 4 to 6 feet from the net).
- Against a quick net rusher (especially if he does not do a split step).[2]
- To charge the net and become offensive (element of surprise).
- When the sun is in you opponent's eyes.
- When your opponent moves slowly or lacks a good overhead.

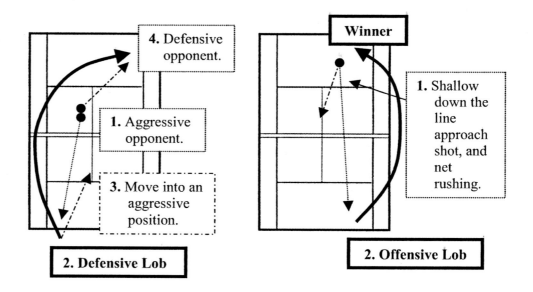

DROP SHOT

- Do not use the drop shot on critical points (15-40).
- Do not overuse it! It works better with the element of surprise (and well disguised).
- Most effective on slower courts (red clay or green "Har-Tru"), and especially when your opponent is well behind the baseline and you are inside the baseline.
- A good drop shot should bounce 3 times in the service box.
- Use it to change pace on a point or to change your opponent's rhythm.
- A very efficient combination against a slower or poorly conditioned player is to make a drop shot and then lob over his head. Also, the drop shot is effective against players who run around the backhand, hitting inside-out forehands, but not aggressively enough (shallow shots).
- Always move up after making a drop shot (covering any possible shot, like another drop shot from your opponent).

How to Read a Drop Shot
- Your opponent holds the forward motion of the racquet (before point of contact) too long.
- Your opponent opens the racquet face as point of contact is executed.
- Anticipate the drop shot by realizing your position (well behind the baseline) with your opponent's position (well inside the court).

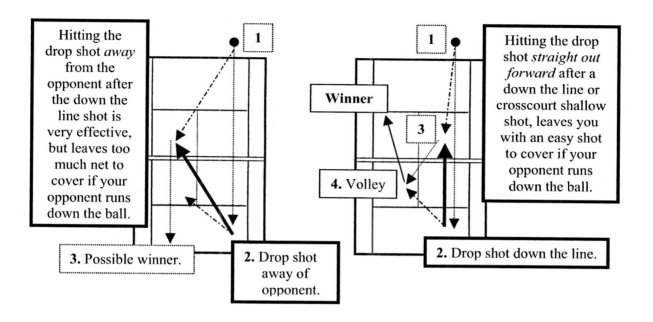

Hitting the drop shot *away* from the opponent after the down the line shot is very effective, but leaves too much net to cover if your opponent runs down the ball.

Winner

Hitting the drop shot *straight out forward* after a down the line or crosscourt shallow shot, leaves you with an easy shot to cover if your opponent runs down the ball.

3. Possible winner.

2. Drop shot away of opponent.

4. Volley

2. Drop shot down the line.

PASSING SHOT

- Placement of the passing shot depends on your position, your opponent's transitional shot placement, and his position in the court. Also, consider your ability to produce a hard shot under pressure and your opponent's ability to move at the net.

- Best passing shots are struck early with authority (at peak of bounce) and low over the net (flat or with heavy topspin).

- Always the quickest is the down the line passing shot. Because the ball covers less distance, the volleyer has less time to react.

- The crosscourt passing shot has a higher percentage of clearance over the net due to crossing over the lowest part of the net (center) and creates less court to cover on any possible opponent's volley.

- When the opponent comes up the middle of the court, a quick low shot into the shoelaces will cut down the probabilities of an angle shot, and, most likely, he will volley up, leaving you to deal with an easy high passing shot.

- Another possibility when the opponent is in a good tactical position (center of reach for your possible passing shot) is to aim directly at him with a powerful drive.

Covering After the Passing Shot

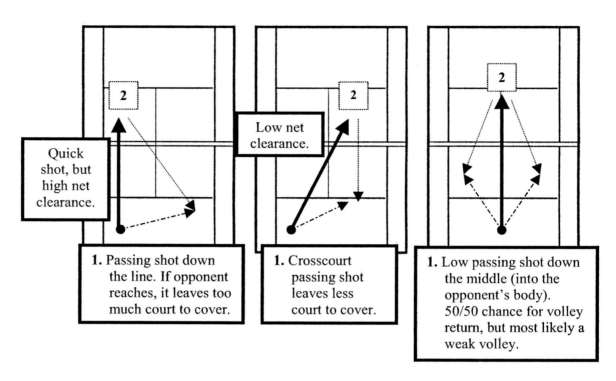

When Hitting a *Cross Court* Passing Shot

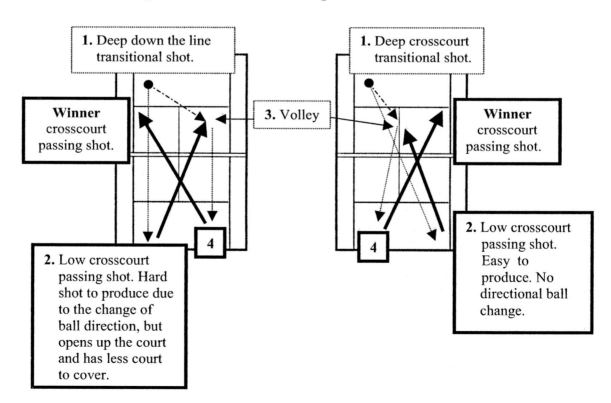

When Hitting a *Down the Line* Passing Shot

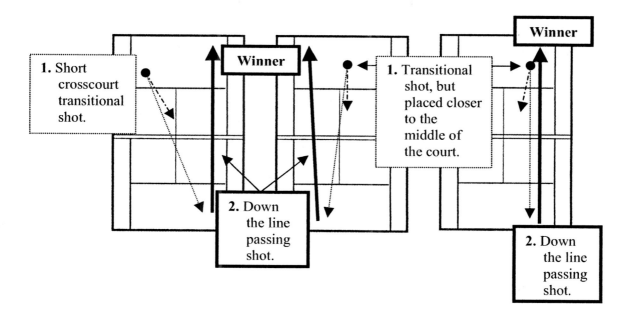

- A *shallow* transitional shot or volley should be attacked down the line (or to the open court), going for a winner or a forcing volley.
- A *deep* transitional shot can also be attacked down the line, but this shot must be selected when the opponent is hesitating, running late (far from net) and/or recovering to the center of the "Ideal Split Area" too quickly, miss-timing the split step.[2]
- Any transitional shot (or net player) can be neutralized with a defensive or offensive lob depending on the situation (player position, player moving forward too fast, and ability to move back).
- Never change your mind when aiming the passing shot, just go for it and force your opponent into a weak volley.

PASSING SHOT VARIATION

ANGLE PASSING SHOT

- A low percentage shot! Choose the right time to perform it.
- Use extreme topspin to hit the target areas and go for a clean winner (spin is the main source of energy. Any extra speed or power on the ball will lower the chance for success).
- Always cover for any possible return.

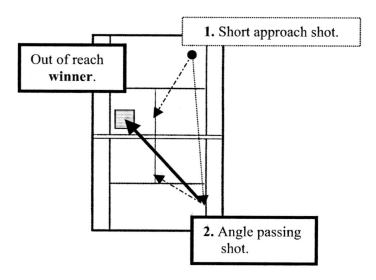

1. Short approach shot.

Out of reach **winner**.

2. Angle passing shot.

ANGLE SHOT

- You opponent must hit a short, wide, close to the sideline shot to produce a sharp angle shot.
- You must use extreme topspin to hit the target areas and go for a clean winner.
- Make sure your opponent is off position or behind the baseline when using this shot.
- Always cover for any possible return.

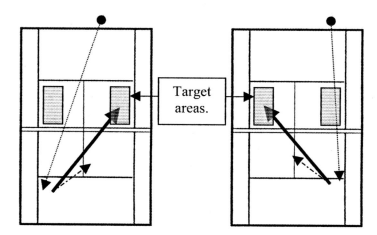

Target areas.

Difference Between a Deep Crosscourt and an Angle Shot

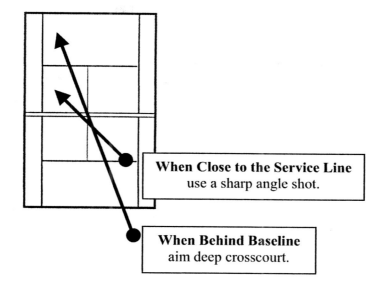

When Close to the Service Line use a sharp angle shot.

When Behind Baseline aim deep crosscourt.

[1] See Chapter 1, **"Spins"**
[2] See Chapter 1, **"Anticipation & Footwork"**

PLAYING THE ELEMENTS

PLAYING THE ELEMENTS

WIND

Playing on windy days is much harder than in normal conditions; but if you include the wind in your tactics, the wind will become a new weapon.

- Shorten up the swings to compensate for the wind factor on the ball.
- Do not make big risky shots by aiming close to the lines.
- Be patient and use high percentage shots.
- Realize how strong the wind is and from which direction the wind blows so you can adjust to it properly.
- Make good footwork a priority to adjust for the wind factor.
- Play high percentage *first* serves. Wind has more effect on spinning second serves.

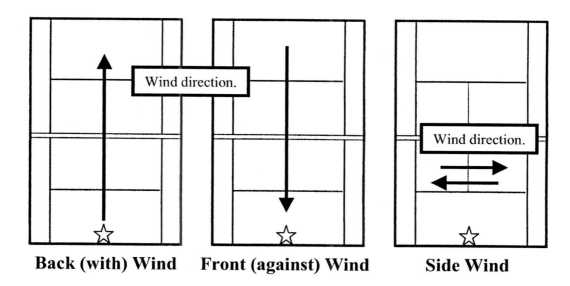

Back (with) Wind   Front (against) Wind   Side Wind

Playing with *Back Wind*

- Wind blows from behind you, carrying the ball deeper, therefore, hit *lower and shorter* than normal.
- Use more topspin on all strokes.
- Attack the net and use the volleys more frequently (a good passing shot gets attenuated by the opponent's front wind).
- Use defensive slice lobs, but consider that the wind will carry that ball deeper than where you are aiming.

Playing with *Front Wind*

- Wind blows against you, slowing down the ball. Therefore, hit *higher and deeper* than normal.
- When long rallies are played and you get tired (since playing *against* the wind requires more energy expenditure than playing *with* the wind), use more angle shots and come to the net to finish up the point quicker.
- Use flatter and harder groundstrokes and serves.
- Use drop shots.
- Use slice with caution (can get short and, therefore, invite your opponent to attack you).
- Use offensive topspin lobs.

Playing with *Side Wind*

- Wind blows from either side across the court.
- Do not aim close to the sideline. Adjust your aiming according to the wind factor.
- Use spin to control the flight of the ball.
- When using a slice serve, measure the wind factor.

SUN

- Use moon-balls and lobs more often when the sun is in front of your opponent's eyes.
- When moon-balls and lobs are used against you, use your free hand to block the sun.
- Adjust toss and stance when serving into the sun.
- "Serve & Volley" only as a surprise element when playing against the sun.

WEATHER AND OTHER CONDITIONS

When playing in different environment (altitude, humidity, indoor, outdoor), acclimatization can take from 4 to 14 days for the body to adapt.

Heat and Humidity

- Humidity limits the effectiveness of body's sweating mechanism. Therefore, consider a lot of fluid replacement.
- If perspiring profusely and playing for more than two hours on a hot day, consider a sport drink which can replace lost minerals and electrolytes (like magnesium, calcium, sodium, and potassium) to avoid muscle cramping.

- If your opponent is in better shape, conserve your energy by not trying to chase out-of-reach shots (usually you should go for everything, even those unreachable ones) or "Serve & Volley" frequently. Come to the net as soon as you can, mostly when your opponent hits a shallow shot. This will make the point shorter, saving you some energy. If your opponent hits deep, use the moon-shot to slow down the pace of the point, thereby, recovering physically (the ball spends more time in the air) and getting to a better position on the court.

Indoor/Outdoor

- Indoor lighting differs from direct sunlight.
- Indoor consistent environment contrasts with outdoor weather conditions.
- Different surfaces (some only indoor).[1]

Altitude

- The higher the altitude, the faster the speed of the ball.
- Greater tendency to hit long.
- Easy to get tired quicker due to difficulty of breathing at high altitude (oxygen load).

[1] See Chapter 5, **"Playing Different Surfaces"**

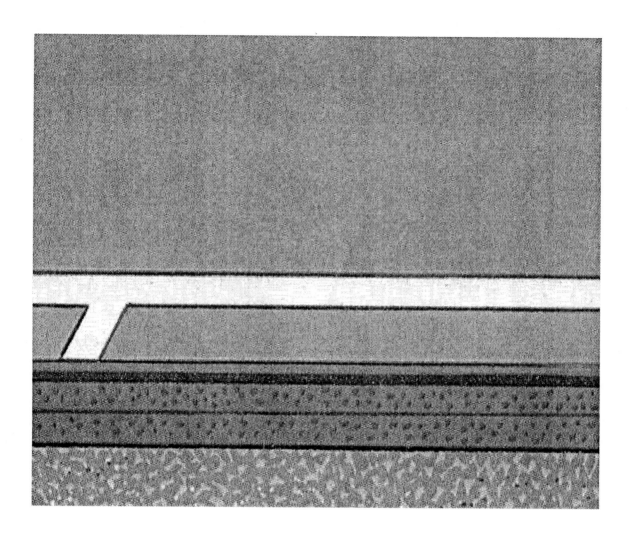

PLAYING DIFFERENT SURFACES

PLAYING DIFFERENT SURFACES

GRASS COURTS

- Construction: very short and compact grass like at Wimblendon, England.
- Court speed: *fast* due to low and unpredictable bounces.
- Low traction, slippery.
- Low impact on knees.
- Strategy: "Serve & Volley" players will dominate the game on this surface. Also suitable for aggressive all court players with a powerful first serve. Quick short points should be the basics of strategy.

HARD COURTS

- Construction: asphalt or concrete usually coated with multiple layers of a mix of acrylic paint and sand.
- Court speed: *fast*. The less abrasive the surface, the faster the court is (the more sand in the mix, the more abrasive).
- Low to medium ball bounce. The smoother the surface, the lower the bounce (ball skids and stays low). Bounce is consistent but depends on surface smoothness and level.
- High impact surface, therefore, hard on knees (most of the impact is absorbed with your legs).
- Best surface for aggressive baseline (with an aggressive first serve), all-court, and "Serve & Volley" players.[1] Because each point happens so quickly, concentration should be a major concern for the player.

CUSHIONED COURTS

- Construction: asphalt or concrete topped with a firm cushioned carpet covered with acrylic and sand mix.
- Most common surfaces are Deco Turf II (US Open), Rebound Ace (Australian Open).
- Court speed: *medium to fast*. Speed of the bounce of the ball depends on abrasiveness of surface coat mixture.
- Medium ball bounce. The ball has more rebound than hard courts due to the resiliency of the cushioned carpet and the roughness of the topcoat. Bounce is more uniform than hard due to consistency of the cushioned layer.

- Easier on the knees than hard courts (the cushioned carpet absorbs some of the shock).
- Hard hitters ("Serve & Volley" players, consistent baseliners) and spin players will benefit from this surface, as well as players with explosive footwork and high level of concentration.

CARPET COURTS

- Construction: rubber-like synthetic or textile carpet on a base of asphalt or concrete.
- Mostly used in indoor courts.
- Court speed: *medium to fast*. Speed depends on material of the carpet. Some textiles are slower than hard. Some synthetics are faster than hard.
- Low to medium ball bounce. Ball tends to have a lower bounce than hard courts. Ball bounce is most consistent. Bad bounces will occur only on old carpets (mostly around the seams).
- Excellent traction. Clay court players will feel that the feet stick to the surface.
- Better than cushioned courts on your knees. Carpet absorbs most of the shock before it transfers up to your knees.
- Best suited for all-court, thinking players (strategy) due to the high consistency of the bounce. Spin is very effective due to the abrasiveness of the surface.

CLAY COURTS

- Construction: a layer of red clay or synthetic green clay is laid over a fine crushed stone base.
- Most common surface in country clubs (indoors and outdoors) in America (green "Har-Tru"). Very popular in Europe, like in the French Open, and South America (red clay).
- Court speed: *slow*. The ball speed is slowed down by the bite of the dust at the bounce.
- High ball bounce. Clay grabs into the ball fuzz and enhances the spin (topspin kicks high, drop shots stays low). Might have some bad bounces due to the surface imperfections from playing. Some shots hitting the lines might also have some unpredictability.
- Sliding footwork techniques are needed.
- Low impact on knees.

- Best suited for patient (expect long rallies), consistent aggressive baseline players and counter-punchers. Spin and depth should be the basics for strategy, as well as good movement, fitness level, and mental toughness.

---

[1] See Chapter 5, **"Different Players"**

DIFFERENT PLAYERS

GAME STYLES: <u>DIFFERENT PLAYERS</u>

Knowing what type of player you are and identifying your opponent's game style will provide a foundation for your strategy in every particular match.

OFFENSIVE GAME (Aggressive Baseline Players, "All-Court" Players and "Serve & Volley" Players / Net Rushers)

Advantages:
- Backcourt aggressive shots, forcing for a weak return or a mistake.
- Aggressive inside out shots to create angle winners, weak opponent's shots, or openings.
- Approach shots put a lot of pressure on your opponent, rushing him into a difficult passing shot as he sees you approaching to the net.
- Volleys shorten up the point by reducing the baseliner reaction time and, therefore, putting your opponent under heavy strain.[1]
- Overheads are put away winners. If you attack the short balls and follow to the net, you have a chance to hit this shot (as well as volleys).
- Constantly changing spins, placement, and pace (drop shots, angle shots, etc.).
- Following a specific strategy or pattern of play, which maximizes your weapons (best shots, usually aggressive play).

Disadvantage:
- Riskier. If your rhythm is off, a defensive player could prevail.

THE AGGRESSIVE BASELINE PLAYER
- Most of the action happens from the baseline, attacking and dictating the point with spin and power.
- Fast and powerful groundstrokes.
- Usually these kinds of players are very quick and will get to any ball, adding pace and depth to the shot.
- Usually they have one strong weapon.

Counterattacking an Aggressive Baseliner

- Be patient and consistent, play more like a retriever with high percentage shots, and let the aggressive player make a mistake as he goes for shots.
- For deep aggressive shots, back up a couple of feet behind the baseline, and shorten up your backswings, feeding from his pace and gaining time.
- If you are more aggressive than your opponent, impose your strength first (dictate the point right from the first shot).
- Find a weakness (usually backhand), and take advantage of it.
- Run around the backhand when possible, but be selective.
- Mix up spins and take pace off the ball with slice shots.
- Come to the net every opportunity you get.
- Attack second serves. Put the aggressive baseliner under attack, forcing him into a defensive mode.
- Bring the aggressive baseliner to the net, lob over his head, and/or force him to volley.

THE "ALL-COURT" PLAYER

- Aggressive and defensive players without a major weapon but possessing an all-around game, who are not afraid to attack the net.
- Good fitness level players.

Counterattacking an "All-Court" Player

- Impose your strength right from the first shot.
- Use percentage tennis and solid game plans.[1]

THE "SERVE & VOLLEY" PLAYER / NET RUSHER

- Quick and agile players.
- Excellent net positioning and coverage.
- Excellent spin serves.

Counterattacking a "Serve & Volley" Player / Net Rusher

- Make sure you focus on the ball, not on the net rusher
- Serve effectively (power, spin, and placement) against a net rusher otherwise he will take command of the point.
- Do not rally with the volleyer. Try to win with one or two quick passing shots.

- Mix up returns, some with no pace and good placement (low into shoelaces), some hard right to the body, and mostly crosscourt (not extremely wide serves).[1]
- Use offensive lob whenever possible.

DEFENSIVE GAME (Retrievers)

Advantages:
- Backcourt steady game.
- Not taking any kind of risk (not attacking the short balls, therefore, no approach shots, no volleys, and no overheads).
- Following a retriever game plan, one more ball over the net. Might also have a specific strategy plan, but its execution and success will depend on the player's ability to control the ball.

Disadvantage:
- The defensive game lets your opponent use his weapons, and, therefore, the offensive player dictates and takes control of the point.

THE RETRIEVER (Counter-Puncher)
- Sometimes called pushers or human backboards. They love to stay at the baseline and return every ball back. They do not use a particular spin, pace or depth, but manage to get it back.
- Some better retrievers or counter-punchers will develop depth and spin, and effectively will use moon-balls (very high and deep topspin shots) as they react to their opponent's game.
- Very consistent, patient, and fit.

Counterattacking a Retriever
- Be patient. Prepare yourself for a long match.
- Do not start pushing the ball yourself; they are kings and queens in that department. Instead, find weaknesses (or a weaker shot) in his game and exploit them (imposing your strength).
- Get to the net on every opportunity you have, even on not so short balls, but be aware of moon-balls.
- Mix up spins and pace. Sometimes they feed from your power. Therefore, some weak shots combined with aggressive shots will take them out of their comfort zone. Also, bring them to the net and lob over their heads or hit some low shoelace shots.

- Focus on closing the point. If you are out of position just put the ball back and deep, as it is unlikely that a retriever will take advantage or your vulnerable position.

[1] See Chapter 5, **"Strategy"**

CHAPTER 6

PREPARING FOR A MATCH

PREPARING FOR A MATCH

STRENGTH TRAINING AND AEROBIC ENDURANCE
Though tennis is a control game, power plays a large role in success. The fitter the player, the longer high performance can be sustained, and, therefore, the higher the chance of accomplishing the task at hand.

Major tennis-specific muscles to consider for *strength training*:[1]
- Shoulder: Anterior, Middle, Posterior Deltoids
- Chest: Pectorals
- Stomach: Abdominals
- Back of Arm: Triceps
- Forearm: Flexors-Extensors
- Back and Lower Back: Latissimus Dorst and Eractors
- Sides: Obliques
- Thigh: Quadriceps
- Back of thigh: Hamstrings
- Calf: Gastrocnemius

For *aerobic endurance*, long-distance runs are ideal. Also, consider treadmills, steppers, bikes, etc.[1]

BALANCE AND AGILITY
Once the strokes are mastered (mechanically sound shots), tennis is mostly a game of strategy and footwork (lower-body). Therefore, quickness and agility are basic ingredients to an effective game, and because most of the shots are hit in motion, good balance is essential.

Balance Drills[1]
- Stand on one foot and maintain balance without wobbling.
- Run on a straight line.
- **Hexagon Drill**

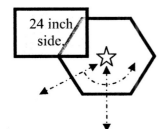

24 inch side.

Standing inside the hexagon, jump over every panel to the outside, and back in immediately, in a counterclockwise direction.

Working on any kind of footwork and anaerobic exercises will benefit your ability to maintain balance, get more agile, and improve quickness.

Footwork Drills[1]
❖ Stress good rhythm and balance throughout the exercise.
- Shuffles: side-stepping.
- Carrioca steps: side-stepping with a cross step in front and one behind.
- High knee jog: jog raising the knees to waist high.
- Butt kick jog: jog kicking your butt with your heels.
- Plyometrics drills: speed and agility drills usually facilitated with cones, ladders, medicine balls, and elastic bands.

Anaerobic Drills[1]
Spider Drill

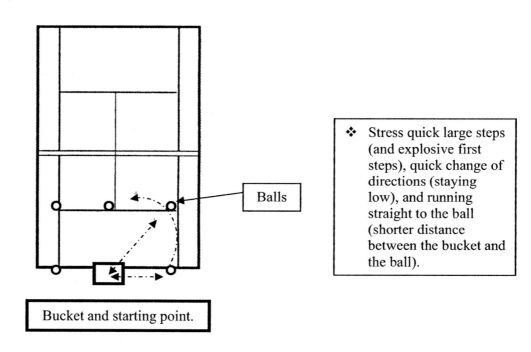

❖ Stress quick large steps (and explosive first steps), quick change of directions (staying low), and running straight to the ball (shorter distance between the bucket and the ball).

Balls

Bucket and starting point.

1. Place 5 balls and an empty bucket (or a racquet) on the intersections of the lines as shown above.
2. Pick up the balls one at a time, in consecutive order, in a counterclockwise direction, placing them into the bucket (or on your racquet instead). Average time for men and women is between 17 to 19 seconds.

Suicide Run

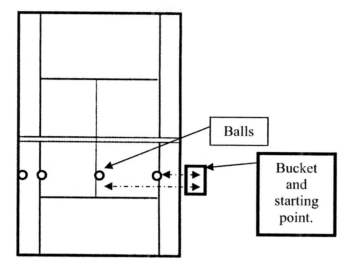

1. Place 4 balls and an empty bucket on the lines as shown above.
2. Pick up the balls one at a time, in consecutive order, placing them into the bucket. Average time for men and women is between 15 to 17 seconds.
❖ Stress explosive first steps and quick change of directions (staying low).

Shuffle, Sprint, Back-Pedal Drill

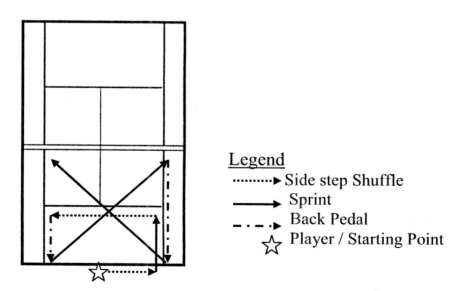

Legend
········▶ Side step Shuffle
——▶ Sprint
— · — ·▶ Back Pedal
☆ Player / Starting Point

1. Follow the lines according to the legend (or make your own pattern).
❖ Stress balance (especially when backpedaling), speed, and rhythm.

KNOWING YOUR GAME

It is essential if you are to win that you know your strengths and weaknesses. Knowing your game will help you map a plan suited to your abilities. Once you identify a strength, work on it until becomes a weapon and then win points by maximizing it. By knowing your weaknesses you can try to work around them, planning a strategy that avoids them.

For an easy identification of your strengths and weaknesses, chart your shots, rate them and plan goals for future improvement.[2]

DATE_____

SHOT[3]	STRENGTH ----▶ WEAKNESS										GOAL
	10	9	8	7	6	5	4	3	2	1	
Forehand											
Backhand											
Volley											
Serve											
Return of Serve											
Overhead											
Approach Shot											
Swinging Volley											
Half Volley											
Lob											
Drop Shot											
Passing Shot											
Angle Shot											
Footwork											
Fitness											
Mental Toughness											

[1] For exercises and specifics on this subject consult a qualified specialist.
[2] See *Charting Future goals* in Chapter 6, **"After the Match"**
[3] Include forehand and backhand sides for all strokes.

<u>BEFORE THE MATCH</u>

BEFORE THE MATCH

GET READY

- Make sure your equipment (racquets, strings, shoes, etc.) is in good condition.
- One to two hours before the match, eat low glycemic-index carbohydrates (maintains blood sugar level for a longer period) like bananas, oatmeal, yogurt, rice, and pasta. Also, include some vegetables and other fruits in your pre-match diet.
- Avoid foods with high sugar content prior to any exercise (due to a quick drop in blood sugar level).
- Have a good night's sleep.
- 30 minutes before the match drink about 250–350 ml. of fluids.

PRESET PLANS

- Preset plans help to build up confidence before the match. At the actual match it will be the foundation of your game. These plans must be refined and adjusted according to each opponent, as you discover his game as the match develops (tactics).
- Every player is different, but determine and practice your preset plans based on your strengths. For example:
  - **Plan A:** I will play aggressively from the baseline, controlling with the backhand and pressing with my forehand, and as soon as I get a short forehand, I will attack down the line and follow to the net.
  - **Plan B:** I will stay at the baseline, using extreme topspin, aiming deep to the center to minimize unforced errors.
  - **Plan C:** I will bring my opponent to the net, lob over his head, mix spins, use angle shots and drop shots.

PSYCHE UP

- Get hungry to win (desire), but do not let your adrenaline control you (high emotions), otherwise, that will interfere with your mental game (state of relaxation during the present moment of a point).
- Have confidence on yourself (expect to perform well, do not just hope to win).
- Use imagery to picture yourself winning points (and specific shots) during that particular match.
- Stay relaxed and positive, confident that you have preset plans to face the opponent (better if you already know your opponent).

PLAYING AUTOMATIC TENNIS
Entering and Staying in the "Zone"

Automatic tennis is a state of mind sometimes called playing in the "zone", where body and mind are linked together in complete harmony, turning the game into automatic reaction, where everything works and a feeling of total enjoyment reigns.

The key elements to enter and stay in the "zone" are:
- Have your mind relax (quiet) by having confidence on your strokes, Preset plans, and a good strategically understanding of the game.
- Use imagery (visualization) to build up more confidence, especially about winning patterns of play (using your strength).
- Disregard the opponent. Play the ball and use targets as you play the point.
- Avoid distractions by concentrating on the ball, especially at point of contact (yours and your opponent's).[1]
- Most important: *Enjoy the moment.*

INJURY PREVENTION[2]

Caution: Stretching without proper warm up (when muscles are cold) may increase chance of injury.

Tennis players require flexibility to play good tennis. Therefore, warm up and stretching becomes essential for all level of players. For injury prevention, **warm up** should be performed ritually *before* the workout and **stretching** *after* the workout (cool down).

Off Court Warm Up

Before hitting any tennis balls, raise your body temperature.
- Light jog around the court.
- Jump rope.
- Jog in place.

Once the body temperature has been raised, do warm up rotations to get the muscles ready for strenuous work.

- **Neck Rotation**
  Do not take the head back, just to the side and forward.

- **Shoulder Rotation**
  A. Arms on the side, make circles with the shoulders as wide as possible. Both directions.

B. Hands on shoulders, make wide forward rotations with the elbows and then go backwards.

C. Arms extended, shoulder level and palm down. First rotate arms in small slow circles, slowly increasing range and speed. Forward and backward. Repeat with palm up.

- ### Hip Rotation
  Hands on hips, rotate trunk without pulling back (to the side and forward). Both directions.

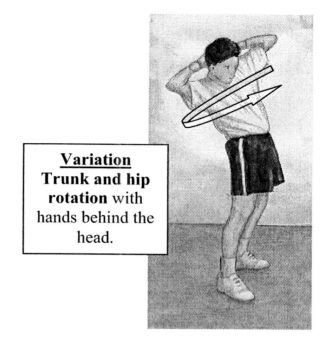

Variation
Trunk and hip rotation with hands behind the head.

- ### Trunk Rotation
  Arms extended to the sides, shoulder level. Rotate trunk to one side and to the other side without lifting the feet (that will tell you how far you should go).

On Court Warm Up

Once a light sweat occurs (warmer muscles can elongate better without injure) start a tennis warm up.

Mini-Tennis

- 3-5 minutes. Mini-tennis is an excellent tool to warm up your strokes before hitting full court. However, sometimes before a match there is a 10 minute time limit, and, therefore, only full court warm up should be performed.
- Mini-tennis is played in the four service boxes, playing full strokes at 20% power.

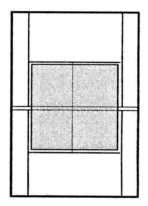

Variations of mini-tennis

Two boxes down the line (one in front of the other). Crosscourt (diagonal) backhands (left to right), and forehands (right to left).

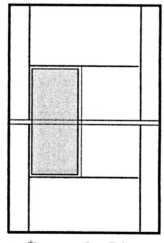 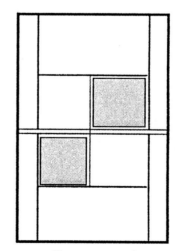

Down the Line   **Crosscourt**

Full Court
- Start at 50% power and slowly increase intensity.
- 5-10 minutes, (groundstrokes, volleys, overheads, and serves).

<u>Major Points to Observe</u> (Identifying Weaknesses)
While warming up, analyze your opponent's game (weaknesses and strengths) in order to plan your strategy.[3]
- Grounstroke preference (running around the backhand).
- Late point of contacts.
- Spins (forehand and backhand).
- Where most errors on groudstrokes occur, at the net or deep?
- Which stance he predominantly uses?
- Does he volley with one or two hands on the backhand side?
- Does he swing at the ball or have a compact punch?
- Does he slice on the overhead or have a flat put-away?
- Does he place the serve or just hit it?
- What kind of spin he controls on the serve (first and second).
- Does he change the toss position when changing spins?
- Is he left-handed or right-handed?

---

[1] See *Focus on the Ball* in Chapter 6, **"While Playing the Game"**
[2] See *Avoiding Injuries* in Chapter 6, **"After the Match"**
[3] See Chapter 5, **"Strategy"**

WHILE PLAYING THE MATCH

WHILE PLAYING THE MATCH

Should You Serve First or Choose Side?
- If you have a good first serve choose to serve to get an early lead. Also, holding the first game carries a psychological advantage because the opponent must hold his game in order to stay in the game (tie).
- If your serve is good, but you feel off rhythm, choose side.
- If your return is better than your serve (and the serve is efficient), choose side. Break your opponent's serve, and then hold your service game. This way you secure the first two games of the set.

DURING THE POINT
- *Take control of the point*: play aggressively the first two shots of each point (serve and first shot, return of serve and subsequent shot).
- *Play automatic tennis*: do not think or talk to yourself while playing the point.
- *Feel relaxed*: enjoy the moment, especially the heat of competition (stay motivated to play, compete, learn, and improve). Let winning be an outcome of performance.
- *Reduce stress* by knowing what you are capable of doing as far as stroke production is concerned (know your game).
- *Maintain a positive attitude at all times*. Remember, confidence is an outcome of winning and performing. Therefore, staying positive and persistent through the matches will eventually help you to achieve results.
- *Play within your limits* (good shot selection) and calculate risky shots.

IN BETWEEN POINTS
Tennis is practically a game of emergencies and pressure. How you handle these situations and the pressure will determine success or defeat. In between points is the critical time to analyze and control all these factors, especially the emotional control, in order to be flexible enough to change or adapt to a new strategy if necessary.

Emotional Control and Adaptability
If a Point Is Won
- Pump up to keep energy high (yeah!, come on!).
- Physical recovery (use several slow deep breaths).
- Plan next point.

If a Point Is Lost

- *Emotional Recovery*

  The most common human reaction is to get down on oneself after losing a particular shot (easy or difficult shot to perform). This kind of behavior is only prejudicial to your performance. You feel bad about yourself, muscles get tight and footwork slows down, mind wanders over the last point and eye vision does not focus on the ball. Therefore, you have a poor performance on the following point. Losing a point is not easy, especially if you really try hard, but be subjective.

  - Do not get down on yourself. Whatever you say (mostly in one word or short sentence), stay positive, saying something that could help you for the following point (ok, keep the pressure, deep, I know what to do, come on!).

  - Think in the present time (next coming point), not the past (maybe just a quick rehearsal of the correct imaginary shot right after the mistake).

  - Analyze the situation and adapt a countering plan.

IMPORTANT POINTS
Game

- If opponent is not strong, get an early lead. Pay attention (play focused) to 30-love or 30-15 advantage. Winning the next point will leave you in a very advantageous position (and especially a psychological advantage).

- If opponent is about your level, play focused on the even point like 30-30 and deuces. If those points are won, that will set you up and give you the confidence to win the game; if not, no harm done, but you will need to work your way back to deuce.

- If opponent is stronger than you, play focused on 15-30 down, so if you get the next point you can feel you are back in the game.

All Sets

- Always win the 1st game (early lead).
- If opponent is not strong focus on the 7th game (middle): 3-3 →
  4-3 → *lead* (then, hold your serving game and you will lead 5-3).
- If opponent is about your level focus at 4-4, 5-5. By winning the following game, you are just one step away from the set (and a significant psycologycal advantage).
- Always concentrate on the last game. Sometimes it is hard to close out the set (or match).

  - Do not change a winning plan. Use the strategy that let you win all those games.

- Maximize your strength and increase margins for error (use more topspin, and aim well inside the lines), but keep dictating the point.
- Make sure your mind does not wander. Keep your mind on the task at hand, based on a solid, sound strategy, and you will stay relaxed and play in the "zone."

Second Set

- Be aware of momentum shifts (if your opponent wins 2 or 3 points in a row, a momentum shift can be created).
- If you won the first set, do not lose your momentum by letting your opponent somehow come back (usually carelessness after winning the first set). Instead, keep dictating your game and adapt to countering any changes in your opponent's strategy (do not forget he wants this set badly after losing the first).
- If you lost the first set, look for an opportunity during the first games of the second set (usually when your opponent relaxes or plays a lazy-loose point). By getting an early lead in the second set, you have a greater chance to take the set.

Tiebreak (12 Point Tiebreaker)

- Get an early lead by dictating your game based on the plan that let you win most of the points, taking also into consideration that a tiebreak requires a solid first serve.
- Playing focused at 5-3 up or down will determine a victory or a comeback.

IF LOSING THE MATCH (during changeovers)

- Analyze the situation (identify the problem) and be flexible to adapt (change tactics or plans).
- *Change Pace*
  - If opponent is hitting aggressively (match is progressing too fast), slow down with floaters (moon-shots) or drop shots.
  - If opponent hits slow pace shots, moon-balls, or inconsistently, attack with volleys, or aggressive shots.[1]
- Aim *deep* with heavy topspin to the center of the court to minimize unforced errors.
- Concentrate on *not losing more than two points in a row*. Once you lose more than two points, your opponent will gain a high level of confidence. By the same token, if you lose two points in a row, try to *neutralize* your opponent with an effective strategy.

- Against a better player, never try to play beyond your limits (over-hitting shots). Play your game while focusing on consistency and percentage.
- Pay attention to your opponent's physical fitness. If you lost the first set, but your opponent is wearing out, keep hitting to the open court, use drop shots and lob him to deplete his energy, and you will have control over the second set.
- Always look for a solution to the situation. The easier way is by asking yourself questions about what you are doing and what your opponent is doing. In other words, you need to find out what your opponent's strategy is, and where he is successful. What is your strategy, and where are you failing? Without knowing this information you will not have too many chances to turn the game in your favor.
- Identify momentum shifts as early as possible. These shifts can happen as you or your opponent win a couple of points in a row, as couples of games are won consecutively, or if one set is won.
- Always drink fluids and, if you get hungry, have a bite of banana, a bagel, a pretzel, or a power bar.

IF LOSING THE RHYTHM
- Keep footwork as a priority (move your feet, keep them active).
- On backcourt rallies split step twice. First, split when the ball bounces at the opponent's side and the second before his point of contact.
- Make sure you get ready to strike the ball (racquet back, get behind the ball) before the ball bounces on your side.
- Make sure you are using all the body links in the right order of execution (sequence, coordination).[3]
- Focus only on the ball and the present point (beware of distractions).
- Impose your game and your strength, disregarding your opponent.
- Play high percentage tennis, using more topspin and not going for the lines.[2]
- Keep a competitive attitude (never give up) at all times, especially when off rhythm.
- Some players will use excessive talk as a tactic to slow down the game or repetitive shoelace tying. They might towel off after each point, taking too much time between points (sometimes the opposite), or make bad calls (honest mistakes and deliberately bad calls). Make sure when any of this happens, you stay focused on your game and strategy, and you keep footwork active (move or skip in place). Never get upset about bad calls. Complain and show that you disagree, and then accept that in every match there will be a certain number of bad calls against you, but that won't make you lose the match.

IF LOSING CONCENTRATION

- Keep your mind in the present time. Do not watch spectators or engage in a conversation with anybody but yourself.
- Use relaxation techniques (see below, "Controlling Anxiety") to stay in or regain the present moment.
- Keep emotions in check (do not get too excited when making a great shot, and do not lament when you make a mistake).
- Do not let a mistake get in your way of winning the following point. Forget about it and move on to the next point.
- Exert extreme effort on every point.
- *Signs of Lack of Concentration*
  - Too many unforced errors (losing games too quickly).
  - Continuously losing track of the score.
  - Thinking of other tasks or issues rather than the present moment.
- *Focus on the Ball* (Eyes Control)
  - Watch the ball leaving your racquet, follow its flight across the net to your opponent's racquet, and follow its way back to you. Continue focusing on the ball in this conscious manner until the point is over.
  - At high-speed tennis, when the ball moves too fast, *focus on the ball when it gets to the peak of the bounce* before you and your opponent makes contact (the ball bounces up, **stops**, and then starts to come down). It is easy to visualize it when it stops.
  - Watch the ball rotation (try to realize its spin).
  - Try to see the seams of the ball, especially at the peak of its bounce.
  - Focus on the bounce of the ball and point of contact by saying at the perfect timing **"bounce"** (when ball bounces on your side)—**"hit"** (when you make contact).

- Know **Your** *Ideal Point of Contact Area* (Striking Zone)

Groundstrokes

> Point of contact is found around waist level, out in front, and on the side of the body.

Volley

> Point of contact is found ideally at eye level, aligned with the front shoulder, and on the side of the body.

Serve / Overhead

 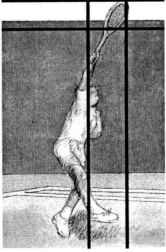

> Point of contact is found high at full stretch, out in front, and on the side of the body.

- To find your point of contact use a grid to consistently meet the ball in the right spot (in space), disregarding spin, speed or placement (running shots) of the ball.
- At high level tennis, when watching the ball at the peak of the bounce is already in the system, and the ball moves at high speed, use the grid technique to focus on the ball without stressing your eyes. Eyes are like camera lenses. When the ball is on the other side at opponent's racquet, your eye focus is in long distance vision. As the ball approaches you, at your point of contact, your eye focus is in short distance vision. Focusing on the ideal point of contact area *before* you make contact, instead of focusing *only* on the ball, will relax you and force you to move better in order to meet the ball in that specific area and, therefore, to play automatic tennis (in the "zone").
- In order to have consistency on all of your strokes (reducing unforced errors) and, at the same time, maintain concentration throughout the point, imagine the grid while hitting the ball. Recognize when you are making contact outside the ideal striking zone grid (especially behind or late).

CONTROLLING ANXIETY

- Do not force yourself to play extremely hard. Work hard on the court (especially footwork), but let it happen. Trying extremely hard will only tighten up your muscles, wearing you out prematurely and slowing you down. Consequently, you will under perform (high muscle tension on the arm will lead to reduced wrist motion and decrease of spin, as well as reduced blood flow and decrease of feel, leading to over-hitting or pushing the ball. Tension in the legs will cause a reduced range of motion, slowing down the effectiveness of your footwork. Mental tension will impair your ability to focus, as well as decrease eye vision sharpness, critically necessary for quick reactions).
- When feeling tight, shake hands, shoulders, or do some neck rotation.
- Try to enjoy, even if the match is not going well (take the hard times with a smile).
- Try to relax at changeovers. If anxiety is high, divert your thoughts from the match. Relax, and you will play better.
- Do several deep breaths (inhaling from the nose, exhaling from the mouth).
- Breathe out when hitting the ball.
- Think only of the present point.
- Think performance over outcome. Always put out 100% effort, and this way anxiety will drop because you are not focusing on the result.

- Believe in yourself and think positively.

- Do not underestimate or overestimate your opponent. Just map your strategy and execute it accordingly. Remember: play the ball, not the opponent.

- Do not be a perfectionist. Let yourself make some mistakes, especially when your opponent hits forcing shots (which differ from your own unforced errors).

- Always move fast (reaction/footwork), but don't rush into hitting the shot (controlling physical anxiety). First, get early in position to hit it and then have a control shot (smooth upper body). Also, as you prepare or hit the ball, do not think what kind of shot you are hitting or about to hit, neither change your mind on any particular shot, during or just before execution (controlling mental anxiety).

Note: Most of the ideas and tips shown in this chapter must to be well practiced before you put them into action, so when you play your match that new information gets incorporated in your game, and, therefore, you can play in the "zone" (automatic tennis).

---

[1] See Chapter 5, "**Different Players**"
[2] See Chapter 5, "**Strategy**"
[3] See *Kinetic Body Chain* in Chapter 1, "**Stances**"

AFTER THE MATCH

AFTER THE MATCH

COOL DOWN

- Stretching while muscles are warm may reduce the risk of injury (increasing range of motion), therefore, always stretch after a workout (cool down).[1]
- Fluid replacement. An adult can lose about 2.5 liters of sweat per hour on a hot day match.
- Eat high-glycemic carbohydrates (allows muscles to recover after exercise) like corn flakes, oatmeal, potatoes, honey, rice cakes, raisins, bagels and breads. Also, some fruits like bananas and oranges are good choices.

Stretching

- Hold the stretch between 20 to 40 seconds.
- Avoid bouncing movements.
- Stretch slowly up to the point of tightness.
- Never feel pain while stretching.
- Focus on staying relaxed (throughout the stretch) while breathing normally.

- **Forearm Stretch**
  Extend arms forward in front of the body. First, pull the palm up with the other hand. After that, push palm down. Repeat stretch with the other arm.

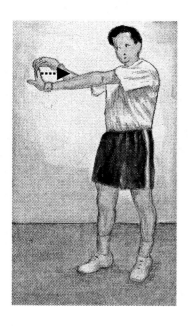 

- **Shoulder Stretch**
  A. Put one arm across the chest, and with the other arm push from elbow towards the chest. Repeat stretch with the other arm.

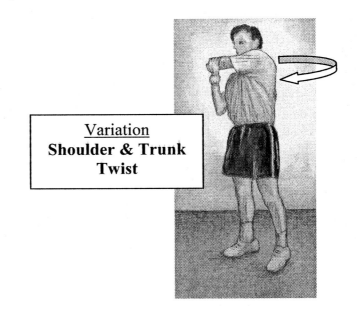

> Variation
> **Shoulder & Trunk Twist**

B. With one arm over and behind the head and the other under and behind the back, try to make both hands meet together (behind back). It can be facilitated with a towel or a racquet. Repeat stretch with the other arm.

- **Hip Stretch**
  Standing with feet shoulder width apart, hold one arm by the elbow behind the head and pull to the side. Switch arms and pull to the other side.

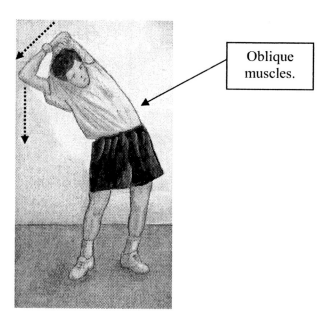

Oblique muscles.

- **Back and Hamstring Stretch**
  Standing with legs straight and feet close together, touch toes with fingertips or as far as possible.

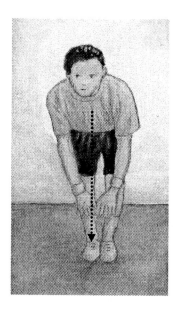

Variations

Feet shoulder
width apart.
Hands to toes.

- **Back, Shoulder, and Hamstring Stretch**
  With hands behind the back interlocked, pull upward as your head pushes downward.

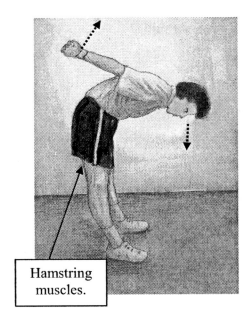

Hamstring
muscles.

- **Groin Stretch**

   Stand with feet wide spread apart. With hands together, bend one knee as far as you can go. The head stays up and body faces forward throughout the stretch. Repeat stretch with the other leg.

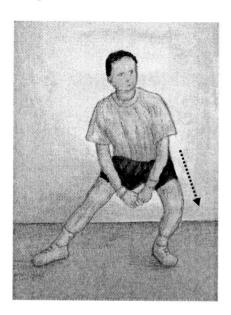

- **Quadriceps Stretch**

   Standing on one leg, hold ankle and pull it to the buttocks. Switch legs.

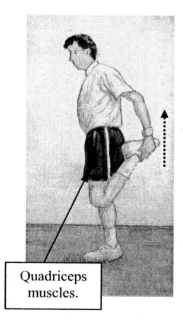

Quadriceps muscles.

- **Calf Stretch**
  Standing straight, facing sideways with the feet widely spread apart, lower your weight down, closing the gap between the back heel and the floor. Repeat stretch with the other leg.

Calf muscles.

Variation
Calf & Groin

Make sure the front knee does not lead the toes.

- **Knee Flexion**

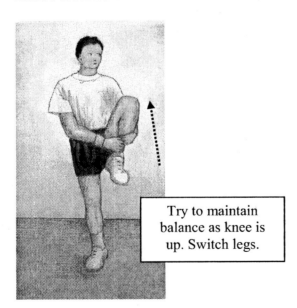

Try to maintain balance as knee is up. Switch legs.

<u>Variation</u>

- **Knee & Spine Flexion**

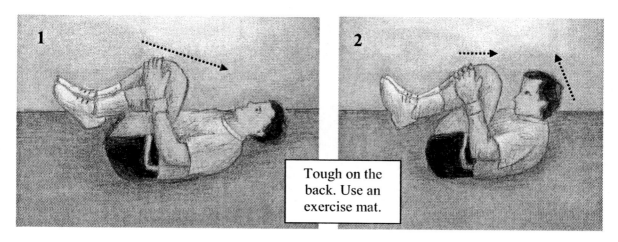

Tough on the back. Use an exercise mat.

- **Hamstring Stretch**
  Sit on the floor with one leg extended forward and other leg bent inward. The knee should touch the floor. Lean chest forward to the extended leg as far as you can (hands grab the extended foot if possible). Switch legs.

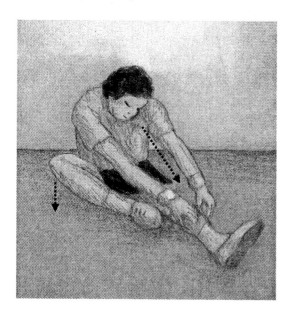

- **Hamstring and Groin Stretch**
  On the floor with legs apart as far as possible, bend from the hip, and try to grab your toes.

- **Lower Back Stretch**
  A. Back Twist
  Sitting on the floor, cross one leg over the other, keeping the knee high (on the crossed leg). Twist back with both arms toward the opposite side of the crossed leg. Switch legs and reverse the stretch.

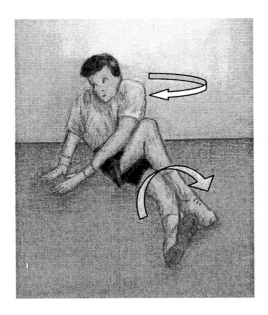

B. Spine Twist

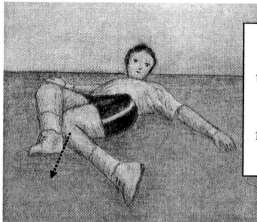

Lying on the floor, cross legs and twist to the opposite side of the crossed top leg (bottom knee to the floor). Concentrate on keeping the shoulders and hips flat on the floor. Switch legs and reverse twist to the other side.

Variations

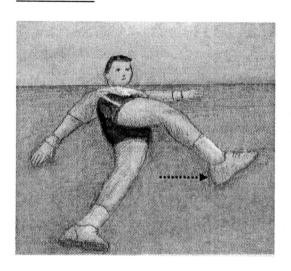 

• Spine Flexion

Push head upward as back is pulled down.

1

Push head downward as back is pulled up.

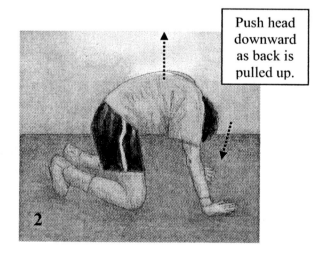

2

<u>Variation</u>

- **Spinal Flexion & Forearm Stretch**

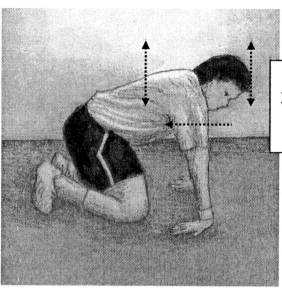

With fingers facing towards you, pull your body backward, flexing the spine (use previous stretch technique for spinal flexion).

- **Inner Thigh Stretch**
  Sitting on the floor, hold the feet together close to the groin. Lean trunk forward as far as you can go, trying to keep the knees close to the floor.

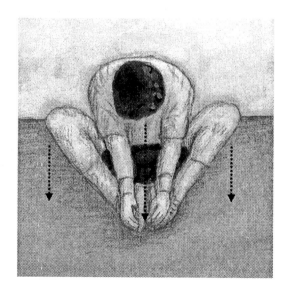

AVOIDING INJURIES

Causes of Injuries

- Poor Technique[2]

  The major goal for any successful tennis player is to have biomechanically sound strokes, not only to play efficiently, but to avoid injury. The basis of biomechanical strokes is to minimize the use of weak muscles, like the forearm (tennis elbow), as well as maximize the use of large group of muscles, like the quadriceps (legs), trunk, and shoulders. These large muscles, used with proper technique, will generate ground forces, which eventually will be the main power transferred into the ball. Also, biomechanically sound strokes facilitate the use of the body links (kinetic body chain) which, together with the ground forces, make stroke production effortless.

- Improper Exercise/Rest Ratio

  Most of the time in any anaerobic training, like tennis, the work/rest ratio should be 1/3. If proper rest time is not enforced, performance will decline, and the risk of injury will be greater.

- Over-training or Abusive Use of Particular Muscles

  Over-training can lead to burnout (physical and mental exhaustion, loss of joy for the game), and any extreme use of particular muscles, without adequate strength training, can lead to injury.

- Age and Capability of Level of Training

  The level of adequate training (conditioning aerobic and anaerobic, flexibility, agility, and strength training) should be determined by a professional, according to your age and overall fitness.[1]

- Inadequate Warm Up Before Extensive Training

  Tennis players perform constant movements, which include sprints, lateral shuffles, jumps, crossovers, and, unlike other sports, tennis requires the whole body for stroke production. Muscles are like rubber bands, when cold and stretched, they may break. Therefore, playing without proper warm up can lead to injury.[3]

LEARNING FROM MISTAKES

Analyzing the Match

The learning process starts by recognizing mistakes and weak spots that your opponent can exploit. After every match, analyze or have somebody charting where the majority of unforced errors occurred. Also, find out what kind of game style you played. Did you follow through with your preset plans? Did you attack the short balls? Did you make forcing shots? Did you find your opponent's weaknesses and exploit them? If you lost your rhythm, did you try to get it back? These are some of the questions that you should be asking yourself after the match.

As for the mental part, did you get nervous? How did you control anxiety? Did you get upset with yourself after a mistake? How was your focus and concentration? Did you have fun (even if you lost the match)? Did you learn something from the match or from your opponent (do not underestimate your opponent)? These are just some questions that you should ask yourself after every match (win or lose). Come up with your own set of questions, and you will see how productive every match will be.

Charting Future Goals

Once you have an idea of what the major problems are in your game or which areas need improvement, write them down as goals to be achieved with specific target dates. You could write short-term goals for something that you want to happen in the next 4-6 months or long-term goals for longer than that. Make sure that these goals are based on performance (physical and mental skills), not outcomes (consequences of performance), and that they are realistic and reachable.

Keeping a goal sheet active and updated will force you to attack and follow a strategy to solve those weak spots of which your opponent always seems to take advantage.

[1] Before engaging into a routine, seek advice from a qualified specialist.
[2] Always consult a professional about proper technique (biomechanically sound strokes). Playing tennis with poor technique can lead to injury.
[3] See Chapter 6, **"Before the Match"**

GLOSSARY

GLOSSARY

AD COURT. The left side of the court when serving, or the box on the left side when receiving. "Ad" short for "advantage," meaning that one player has an advantage. Points played on this side: 0-15 / 15-0, 15-30 / 30-15, 30-40 / 40-30, and ad-in / out.

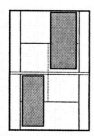

ANGLE OF INCIDENCE. The angle that a ball makes **"A-B-C"** with the normal (perpendicular) **"B-C"** when it bounces on the surface.

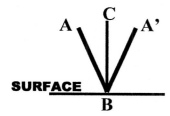

The angle of reflection **"A'-B-C"** must be taken into consideration in order to judge the point of contact correctly on all types of groundstrokes and especially on overheads hit with the bounce. *Note*: A-B-C = C-B-A'

ANGULAR MOMENTUM. The angular force generated by the body as it rotates forward to the point of contact.

AUTOMATIC TENNIS. State of mind sometimes called playing in the "zone," where body and mind are linked together in complete harmony, turning the game into automatic reaction, where everything works and a feeling of total enjoyment reigns.

BACKCOURT. The area formed between the baseline and an imaginary line 4 feet behind the service line.

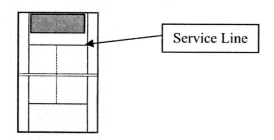

BACKSWING.   The taking of the racquet backward to prepare for its forward motion.

BASELINER.   A baseline player. A player who spends most of his game around the baseline or backcourt.

BODY LINKS.   See "Kinetic Body Chain."

CENTER OF GRAVITY.   Imaginary point where body weight is evenly distributed.

CENTER MARK.   Little mark on the baseline showing the middle of the court.

CHANGE OF PACE.   Shots stroked at different power levels (and spins), in order to upset the opponent's timing, rhythm, and concentration.

CHIP & CHARGE.   Referring to a "Chip" return of serve (see chapter 2 "Return of Serve" variation "The Chip") and following to the net (charge) as a strategy or style of play.

COILING.   Sometimes called "Elastic Energy, Loading-up, or Pre-stretch". Energy stored in muscles as a consequence of stretching those particular muscles, like the turning of the shoulders to prepare for a groundstroke.

CONCENTRATION.   The ability to maintain attention over a period of time. Most important skill to achieve at high level tennis in order to attain maximum performance (automatic tennis).

COMFORT ZONE.   The area in space where most likely the racquet and the ball will meet at point of contact. See also "Striking, Power, and Hitting zone".

CROSSCOURT.   A shot directed across the court (diagonal).

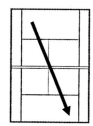

DEUCE COURT.   The right side of the court when serving, or the box on the right when returning. The points played on this side are mostly the even numbers: 0-0 or love-love (the start of the game), 15-15, 30-30, 40-40 (deuce), and 15-40 / 40-15.

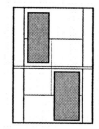

DOWN THE LINE. A shot hit parallel and close to the sideline.

DRIVE. An aggressive deep shot (forehand or backhand) stroked with mostly topspin or flat. A forcing shot.

DYNAMIC BALANCE. The ability to maintain equilibrium while the body is in motion.

EXTENSION. Increase of the angle produced by two body parts, like the straightening of the knee (from a flexed position) to produce ground forces.

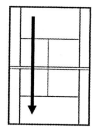

FOLLOW THROUGH. The continuation of the racquet right after the point of contact.

FORCING SHOT. An offensive shot (mostly drives) that forces your opponent into a defensive situation (or a weak shot).

FREE ENERGY. Referring to weight of the body. Used in conjunction with the "kinetic chain" to add power and efficiency to the strokes.

GAME PLAN. A strategy that is carefully thought-out beforehand, based on your strengths and weaknesses and some other conditions (surface, weather, wind, indoor, outdoor, level of fitness, etc.).

GRAVITY. Downward acceleration. The force of attraction by which terrestrial bodies tend to fall toward the center of the earth.

GROUND FORCE. The force generated from the ground as the body (legs extension) pushes off against it. See also "Kinetic Chain".

GROUNDSTROKE. A forehand or a backhand. Referring to a stroke that is hit after the bounce, usually on the backcourt.

HEAVY SHOT (HEAVY BALL). A powerful fast shot that carries a heavy amount of topspin.

HITTING ZONE. The area in space where most likely the racquet will impact the ball (point of contact). See also "Striking, Power, and Comfort zone".

HYPEREXTENSION. The bending backwards of the hand at the wrist (wrist laid back), creating a valley between the back of the palm and the forearm.

INERTIA. The tendency objects have to resist changes in their state of motion (sliding after stopping on clay courts).

INTERNAL ROTATION. Forward (internal) rotation of the arm from the shoulder socket as the racquet moves to the point of contact and follow through on groundstrokes.

KINETIC BODY CHAIN. The segments of the body that act as a chain (body links) in order to produce energy. Starting with the knee extension, ground forces are generated, and successfully transferred from link to link until they reach the ball. The body link system consists of (in order of execution): Knee extension → hip rotation → trunk rotation → shoulder and arm rotation → elbow extension (internal rotation) → wrist flexion.

LINEAL MOMENTUM. The linear force generated by the body weight as it is transferred forward to the point of contact.

LOOPING SHOT. A high-flying shot that reaches around 6 to 8 feet over the net, usually hit with topspin. Looping shots are mainly used to clear the net with higher percentage, especially when under attack. See also "Moon-shot."

MENTAL TOUGHNESS. The ability to maintain a stable mental state (emotions, concentration, motivation, and thoughts) under pressure for a period of time (throughout the match).

MOMENTUM. Force or energy generated by the body. See "Linear or Angular momentum."

MOON-SHOT. A high shot, higher than the looping shot, that reaches around 8 to 10 feet over the net, usually hit with topspin, but doesn't have the height of a lob. Moon-shots are mainly used to keep the opponent deep, as well as a recovery strategy. See also "Looping shot."

NO-MAN'S-LAND. Area in the middle of the court, between service line and the backcourt.

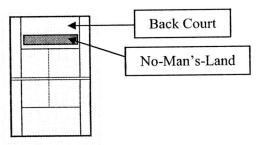

PACE. A combination of speed and power generated from the ground up (see "kinetic chain") and transferred into the ball.

PERCENTAGE TENNIS. Strategy that uses spin, geometry of the court, and player's position in the court as foundation to win points.

POINT OF CONTACT. The moment that the strings make contact with the ball.

POWER ZONE. The area (in space) where most likely the racquet and the ball will impact at point of contact. See also "Striking, Hitting, and Comfort zone."

PRONATION. Rotation of the palm inward and out on the serve and overhead (from a thumb up position at point of contact to a thumb down position) right after point of contact (on the follow through).

RALLY. To keep the ball in play, back and forth, for a consecutive number of times.

RETRIEVER. A defensive player usually with high level of fitness who relies on a strategy of returning every ball (like a wall), forcing his opponent to miss the shot or to make a tactical mistake.

RHYTHMICALLY SOUND SHOT. A stroke founded on the principles of biomechanics and optimum technique.

SHORT BALL. A ball that bounces around the service line that can easily be attacked.

SLICE SPIN. Same as underspin on a stroke or sidespin on a serve.

STORE ENERGY. The pre-stretching of the muscles when coiling the body, in preparation for a stroke. *Example*: the turning of the shoulders on the backswing of a groundstroke.

STRIKING ZONE. The area (in space) where most likely the racquet and the ball will impact at point of contact. See also "Hitting, Power, and Comfort zone."

STRATEGY. A general plan or method to ensure a specific goal (victory). Also a style of play.

TACTIC. The procedure of maneuvering the strategies or strengths in order to achieve a specific result. Fine adjustments of the basic strategy counterattacking the opponent's strategy.

TOUCH SHOT. A delicate, controlled shot, hit mostly with a loose wrist (and hand) to produce drop shots, drop volleys, and some angle shots.

TRAMPOLINE EFFECT. Referring to the racquet strings. When the strings are loose (low tension) and the ball leaves the strings after the point of contact, the speed of the ball is increased because of that deflection effect.

UNIT TURN. Initial upper body rotation (shoulder turn) that occurs, as racquet is prepared for a stroke on the backswing.

UNFORCED ERROR. A non-forced mistake.

VOLLEYER. A volley player.

WRIST SNAP. Flexion of the wrist at the end of the stroke. Last body link of the kinetic chain power production.

ZONE. Referring to "playing in the zone." See "Automatic Tennis."

COURT DIMENSIONS (*Top View*)

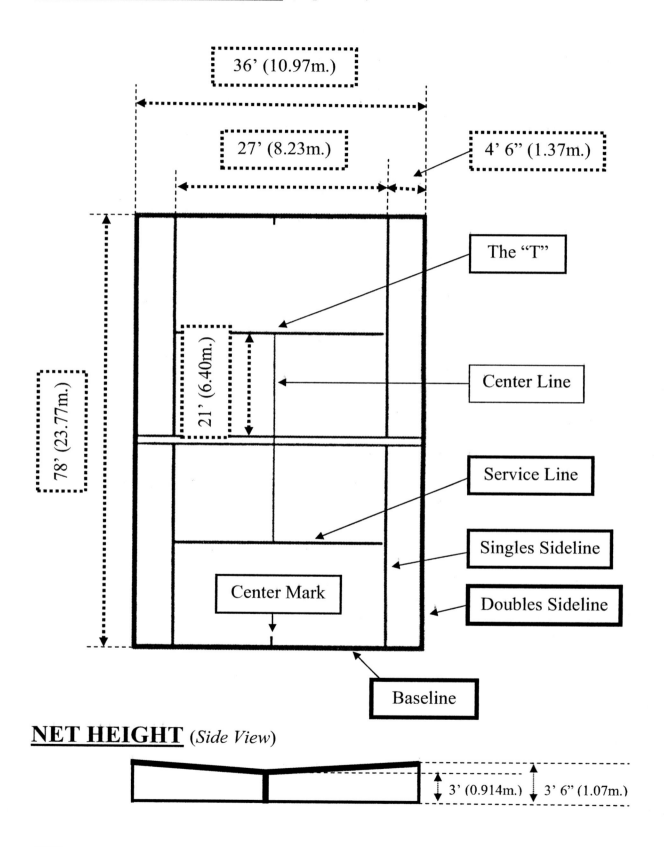

36' (10.97m.)

27' (8.23m.)

4' 6" (1.37m.)

The "T"

Center Line

21' (6.40m.)

78' (23.77m.)

Service Line

Singles Sideline

Center Mark

Doubles Sideline

Baseline

NET HEIGHT (*Side View*)

3' (0.914m.)   3' 6" (1.07m.)

FINAL WORDS

Since I was a young kid, my life has revolved around tennis. Most of my friends knew what they wanted to be when they grew older. Some wanted to be doctors, some lawyers—you know, the usual—but not me.... I wanted to be a tennis player. What kind of profession is that, anyway? I could not answer that question myself. As a young adolescent, I still had no clue what I would be if I did not become a tennis player, and because of that my life revolved around only tennis. I was always proud of my efforts, in victory and defeat. Every night I would come home from training with a new blister in my hand...and I was happy, feeling I was fulfilling my dream.

Well, life on the tour was not easy, especially without financial support, so after trying for a couple of months, I realized that I could not be the greatest player in the world as I had dreamt of being. Consequently, I left the tour and started reflecting on my future. I did not know much about anything but tennis. I tried to follow a career. I became a chef, which I loved, but that did not last. So, I went back to college, becoming a biochemist. Still, deep inside my heart there was only one thing for me, the love of the game, the challenge that every stroke every day could bring, and the desire to become a better player every time I stepped on the court. And so, I discovered that I did not need to get away from tennis to survive. Today I am the happiest person on earth knowing that my tennis career is not at an end...but at a beginning.

Julio Yacub

RECOMMENDED READINGS
Classic Tennis Handbook, by Nick Bollettieri
Mental Tennis, by Vic Braden and Robert Wool
Sports Nutrition Guidebook, by Nancy Clark
Winning Ugly, by Brad Gilbert and Steve Jamison
Tennis for Advanced Players, by Jack Groppel
USPTR Manual, Volume III, Mental Toughness Training, by Jim Loehr
Tennis Tactics, Winning Patterns of Play, by the USTA
Complete Book of Tennis, by Dennis Van Deer Meer

RECOMMENDED VIDEOS
"Nick Bollettieri Video Series" by Nick Bollettieri
"Vic Braden Sports Instruction Video Collection" by Vic Braden
"The Competitive Edge" by Jack Groppel

ABOUT THE AUTHOR

Julio Yacub, B.Sc., is a native of Buenos Aires, Argentina and holds a B.Sc. in biochemistry with specialties in DNA research and human movement. He has been playing tennis for over 30 years and has an extensive experience in teaching and coaching. Yacub is a USTA "High Performance Coach," and a member of the U.S. Professional Tennis Association and the Professional Tennis Registry for more than 10 years.

Julio's driving-force motto—"Never too late to learn"—takes him all around the world to participate in tennis workshops and conventions, constantly acquiring new knowledge and then passing it into the development of his students. Currently he is a speaker, private coach and senior pro at Eastern Athletic Club in Dix Hills, New York.

ABOUT THE ARTIST

Henche Silberstein, is an impressionist painter and writer. Brought up and educated in Buenos Aires, Argentina, Henche studied art in school and privately. With her natural talent and inspired by the harmony and beauty of nature, Henche has created lively canvases that were displayed in numerous art galleries around the world. She lives in Long Island, New York, and even though she has retired from the art world, she continues to paint and write.

<u>INDEX</u>

A

B

C

G

H

I

J

K

L

The opportunity to grow is more enjoyable when shared!
You can contact me at yacub@tenniscoachonline.com
or visit my website at
www.tenniscoachonline.com

Printed in the United States
59126LVS00005B/4

9 781587 362125